To Felix
With Best Wishes
Jerry Hawthorn

Motorcycling Through History During The Golden Age of Postcards

by Jerry S. Hooker

This edition published in 2004 by
Motorcycle Memories
757 Brushwood
Walled lake, MI 48390
All orders and correspondence to this address.

This book was conceived and published by
Jerry Hooker
Motorcycle Memories
www.motorcycle-memories.com

Text by Jerry Hooker
Design by Jerry Hooker
All postcards shown, property of Jerry Hooker

ISBN 0-9748608-0-8
Copyright © Jerry Hooker, 2004
First printing 2004

All rights to this book are reserved. No part may
be reproduced or transmitted in any form or by
any means electronic, mechanical, photocopying,
recording or by any information storage or
retrieval system without the written permission
of the author.

Proudly printed in the U.S.A.
on acid free paper.

CONTENTS:

DEDICATION / ACKNOWLEDGEMENTS — 4

INTRODUCTION: — 5

CHAPTER I: AMERICAN CYCLES — 9

CHAPTER II: EUROPEAN CYCLES — 41

CHAPTER III: RACING — 71

CHAPTER IV: SIDECARS — 83

CHAPTER V: ADVERTISING — 97

CHAPTER VI: HOLIDAYS — 109

CHAPTER VII: MILITARY — 139

CHAPTER VIII: HUMOROUS — 165

APPENDIX: POSTCARD RESOURCES — 246

BIBLIOGRAPHY: — 247

INDEX: — 249

DEDICATION:

This book is dedicated to my lovely wife Sheila, who has stood by me through all of my attempts to make a little extra money from my collecting passion. Should that ever happen, I pray that the shock will not be too great for her. In the meantime, her hearty laughter keeps me from taking things too seriously. And to my wonderful daughters, Susan and Jessica who may at times question my madness, this book is for you, not that you will want it. And finally to Aaron, my first grandchild, and his cousin, Samuel, may you grow up to have an appreciation for all things of historic value, and a curiosity about those things and people that came before you.

ACKNOWLEDGEMENTS:

Although this book has been mostly a one person effort, there are others who have helped in one way or another, especially my daughter Susan who graciously provided her formatting skills to guide me in keeping the page layout of this book looking professional. To all of those people who have saved these post card mementos and made them available to me, I am grateful. In particular I want to thank Ron De Bijl from The Netherlands, who for many years has saved motorcycle related cards and made them available to me on a first choice basis before offering them for sale elsewhere. Many of the cards that came from the Netherlands were supplied by him.

I also want to thank all those individuals who helped with identifications and translations which has enhanced the value of this book. A last minute thank you is also extended to Mike Price who graciously provided his postcard expertise and proof reading skills to point out some errors caught during a fast read over supper, two days following the book going to the printer, but not too late to make corrections.

A special thank you is given to Lee Ann Hole who provided the web site design that has made it possible for me to reach collectors and enthusiasts around the world.

LA GRAPHICS & DESIGN
Graphic and Web Design
www.lagraphicsonline.com

INTRODUCTION:

It is doubtful that many collectors start collecting with the idea in mind that eventually a book will evolve. I certainly did not begin with that intention. For me, postcard collecting began innocently enough, when in 1995 I purchased a card at a flea market in England. I had never thought about collecting postcards, but as long as I can remember, I have been fascinated with motorcycles. Eventually postcards and motorcycles came together and a passion was born. That first card-a studio photo of a couple on an early Triumph cycle-lit the fire that has driven me to a passion for collecting and documenting early motorcycle history as seen through the postcard medium.

Postcard collecting is a worldwide hobby with dealers continuously participating in shows and exhibitions. Collectors gather at these events in search of some new addition for their collections. Since the advent of the Internet, the world has opened up to this area of collecting. Light in weight and often inexpensive, postcards are an ideal area of collecting.

In the "Golden Age" of postcards, that period between 1898 and 1918, millions, if not billions of postcards were produced in every conceivable subject area. Sending and collecting became a national craze. Certainly vast amounts of these cards never survived, still these small mementos from family and friends were often treasured and kept safe in scrapbooks or other albums. Today they are finding their way into the hands of a great number of collectors who maintain personal collections or buy and sell as a hobby or profession.

A great many books have been written on the subject and periodicals abound that cater to the field of Deltiology. The Deltiologist, or postcard collector as they are less formally known, tend to specialize in certain areas of collecting. It would be impossible to specialize in too broad a range of subject matter due to the vast amounts of material available and like anything else, the costs involved. Postcard collecting does not have to be very expensive unless a subject area has been chosen where there is great competition for the relatively few choice items available.

As my collection grew, I saw the possibility of sharing it with other interested postcard collectors as well as vintage motorcycle enthusiasts. Although it may seem to be an unlikely sharing of interests, both groups are drawn to the material and often from diverse viewpoints.

This book is a small attempt to portray the type of historical material that is available on the subject of motorcycles. It is representative of the material published in the first third of the 20th century. Undoubtedly there are hundreds or even thousands of other images in circulation that focus on motorcycles. If I live long enough, perhaps I will add a few hundred more examples to my collection and they can be included in future editions of this book.

The intent of this book is to help document the early history of motorcycling in the first four decades of the 20th century. The motorcycle and its owners have traveled through decades of varying degrees of acceptability. Initially motorcycles were practically a necessity and the only economical way a family had to travel at any speed greater than a horse. Even in those early days, a few riders could be counted on for making too much noise or terrorizing people and farm animals. Eventually, the motorcycle took on rebel appeal which was brought to national attention in 1947 when some 4000 bikers roared into Hollister, California and partied a little too hard. This event was brought to the cinema in 1954 with Marlon Brando and Lee Marvin starring in the movie, "The Wild Ones", a recreation of the events in Hollister. The negative image that was born in Hollister has not completely disappeared, but great strides towards acceptance have been gained in the last few decades.

When Soichiro Honda introduced America and the world to a new kind of motorcycle, a different age was born. "You meet the nicest people on a Honda" became an advertising slogan that captured the imagination of enthusiasts everywhere. After the 1950s and 1960s when riding a motorcycle meant owning an Indian, Harley-Davidson or some loud British machine, and dressing in black leather, the image of the motorcyclist started to become more acceptable.

The growth in the interest of motorcycles has been phenomenal and it has again become an accepted "family" sport. Racing and sport riding are at their height of popularity and sidecars have seen a resurgence of interest. With cruising machines as powerful as they are, it is common to see whole families on the highway pulling sidecars or trailers or both.

With the vintage postcards in this book we can look back at the roots of motorcycling and marvel at how far the sport has come. Who back then would have imagined that the modern motorcyclist would be navigating with the help of a global positioning system made possible by satellites revolving around the earth? Or could that earlier rider have imagined heated grips and seats or an onboard CD changer?

It is interesting to note how little has really changed. If you look at today's technology, the basics were all there one hundred years ago. Refinements have been made and accessories added that would never have been thought of in the first part of the last century. As early as 1907 there was a motorcycle with eight cylinders that exceeded 135 Mph. There were machines with shaft drives and liquid cooling, as well as suspensions that did a pretty good job considering the roads that were available. Cross country touring was not uncommon and coast to coast records were constantly being broken. Machines were definitely less complex then and generally speaking, the average rider had to know how to maintain and repair his own motorcycle. The complexity of today's machines has taken away some of the intimacy that early riders had with their cycles. Perhaps that is not all bad, but many of us think that the basics are still good enough.

A great effort has been made to properly identify the motorcycles depicted throughout this book. I do not claim to be an expert regarding antique motorcycles, and with limited resources I have tried to be as accurate as possible. Errors have undoubtedly been made and corrections are eagerly accepted. Where text translations have been given, they were provided by many sources and are believed to be accurate.

In some cases logos or other graphics pertaining to various motorcycle manufacturers have been inserted into the text. I have done this to add historical interest and they are not a part of the original postcard. Details and distinguishing features that are part of the original postcard are shown next to many of the photo's. It is my intent to show some of the of unique features of postcard design.

An important part of early postcards were the stamp boxes. Many times they served to identify a publisher or to indicate the amount of postage required. Dating postcards can be done to some degree by knowing when various stamp boxes were used. Examples are shown throughout this book as well as the original postmark or stamp when available.

This book is not intended to be a how-to on collecting postcards or a price guide to individual values. With prices fluctuating continuously based on supply and demand, a price guide has limited value. A far more practical approach is to watch the auction sites and subscribe to postcard publications that track sales on a regular basis. Another way is to attend postcard shows that are continuously held around the world. The mass produced publisher cards are generally more available than the real photo cards that often were printed in small quantity for family and friends. In some cases I have noted when a particular card is especially rare.

In judging the rarity of postcards with a motorcycle theme, I have but my own experience and observations to draw upon. The opinions are my own, based on years of watching the market for these collectible cards. In general I have found the following guidelines to be true in the current market.

- Any motorcycle card with a sharp, detailed, real photo image prior to 1910 is in high demand and considered quite valuable. Expect to pay in the $ 50.00 to $ 100.00 range. Later dates bring $ 35.00 to $ 75.00.
- Those cards showing an obscure make of motorcycle are the most prized, particularly American cycles, but also European. Expect these to range from $35.00 to $ 100.00.

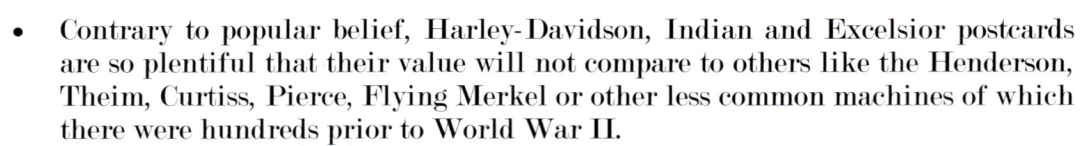

- Contrary to popular belief, Harley-Davidson, Indian and Excelsior postcards are so plentiful that their value will not compare to others like the Henderson, Theim, Curtiss, Pierce, Flying Merkel or other less common machines of which there were hundreds prior to World War II.
- Sharp, side view photo's are much preferred over front-on views.
- Early photo's of women on motorcycles are often more valuable than those of men due to much less availability.
- Cards with a racing theme especially board track racers in clear close up views are very valuable often running from $ 50.00 to $ 100.00.
- Mass produced cards by known publishers, to include those in categories of humor, advertising, holidays or military, generally hold less value than the real photo cards.
- One particular exception to the lower value of mass produced cards are advertising cards featuring a particular motorcycle. These are very desirable and bring high prices generally from $ 35.00 to $ 75.00.
- Cards featuring Santa Claus on a motorcycle attract a variety of collectors and will often command high prices, especially the less common ones. The rarest ones can bring over $ 100.00, but most fall in a range below $ 50.00
- Postcards with motorcycles and an Easter theme seem to go well together especially in the European countries where they are very common. Typically they do not command very high prices and can be found in the $ 10.00 to $ 30.00 range. American, Easter / motorcycle cards are rare.
- Cards with a humorous content are generally the least valuable of the motorcycle categories. The majority fall into the $ 5.00 to $ 25.00 range.
- Like any collectible, condition plays a big part in a card's value. Less important to the value is whether a card has been posted. In many cases that is preferable especially when a clear postal cancel is available. Damage to the image side of the card will most dramatically affect it's value.

Remember, regardless of what you think a card is worth, it will bring only as much as someone is willing to pay at a particular moment in time. If buying, do not hesitate to negotiate price. If selling, watch the market and be realistic in your expectations and research what you have.

CHAPTER I: AMERICAN MOTORCYCLES

Motorcycling Through History

The Laughing Indian card is a much sought after postcard and is frequently found on auction sites. It dates from 1909 and was used to advertise the Indian Motocycle. This particular card was distributed by the Renner Repair Co., New Midway, MD. selling agent for Indian Motocycles. American Indians were used as symbols for the Indian Motocycle Co. and it's agents. The front fender ornament became an Indian head in later years.

LIKE A FLASH
INDIAN MOTOCYCLE
HENDEE MFG. CO.
SPRINGFIELD, MASS.

This photo from 1921 depicts two Native Americans who helped promote the Indian Days celebration, a yearly event held by many Indian dealers. The occasion of this photograph was the celebration at the Badger State Motorcycle Co. in Milwaukee, WI. The motorcycle is probably a "PowerPlus model" and is attached to a "Flexit" sidecar.

From the ca. 1909 Indian at the top of this page to the 1941 model shown here, one can see the great advances that were made. *"Just arrived in town! The new 1941-40th anniversary Indians, featuring a brand new Sport Scout "45" with individually sprung front and rear wheels — new all chrome sealed beam headlights— new super sports type engines.. This card is our special invitation to you to come in and look'em over. Bring your friends."* "Teknitone by Colourpicture, E.B. Thomas, Cambridge, Mass.

1941 *Indian* "45"
Featuring THE NEW "DOUBLE ACTION" SPRING FRAME

10

Chapter I: American Cycles

Seen here is a relatively common postcard found fairly often on auction sites. It is quite desirable and promotes the wholesome family nature of motorcycling. This card was posted on May. 6, 1916. The styling of the motorcycle is consistent with that time period. The card was sent to Miss Mildred Thompson at Yellow Springs OH.

A very rare card is this one with a Scottish flavor. It was posted from Stoke-On-Trent, England to Stafford England. The date is 22 Feb. 1918. A postal cancel encourages buying war bonds. The motorcycle could indeed be representative of a 1918 model. *"Bain't you afraid to ride it Missy? No it's so simple."*

On April 21, 1914, this card was posted to Roseburg, Oregon. On the gas tank preceding "Indian" is the numeral 20 and following the name is the No. 1. The significance of this is not known. The caption seems to say "just leave me alone, I can ride this thing." For women at the turn of the last century riding a motorcycle was quite daring, but many took to the adventure and became skilled. See card on page no. 188.

11

Motorcycling Through History

Some early examples of Indian motorcycles are shown on this page. Here is a wonderful card posted Mar. 31, 1910 from York, Nebraska. It was produced by Huffman's General Supply House, Mfrs. Photographic local views, York, Neb. The Indian shown is probably a 1909 model equipped with a rear passenger seat and a handlebar seat for the lovely young ladies.

At right is another very nice card that contrasts the old and new modes of transportation. The model shown is probably a very early 1910 machine including the leaf spring front suspension that was new that year. Sitting on the cycle is Clark Fleming and behind him is Jesse Fleming in the buggy. Information supplied with the card says the photo is 1914. The photo is by W.C. Caldwell, Humboldt, Kansas.

This beautifully clear photo shows a ca. 1913 Indian. An identifying feature is the rear leaf suspension that was introduced that year. This card was never used and is very clean. From the writing on the front of the card it cannot be determined where "Home" is located. Unfortunately the author's writing is not clear.

12

Chapter I: American Cycles

The Indian motorcycle Co. began in 1901 When George M. Hendee and Oscar Hedstrom collaborated on a design for a motor driven bicycle. Their earliest designs, up until the 1908 models all had diamond shaped frames. Later designs became stronger, loop frames. The cycle in this photo is probably a 1905-1908 model. Could the rider be the G.P. Smith from the store behind? Any pre-1909 Indian postcards are highly desirable and difficult to find.

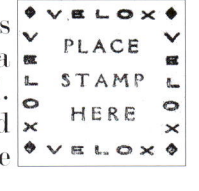

The Indian in this photo appears to be a post-1905 model. Again, the rider and any other details are unknown.

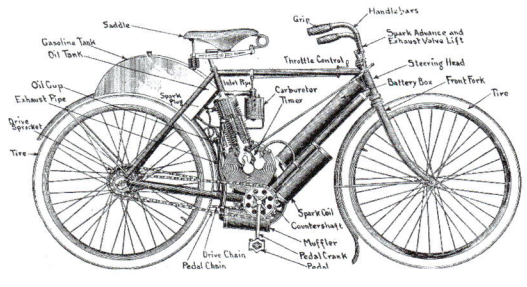

This young man proudly sits atop a new 1909 Indian. Note the loop frame. The round coil spring suspension on the front fork tube lasted until the 1910 models which came with a leaf spring. The "Camel Hump" gas tank has been replaced with a more conventional design. This card was sent to Mr. Mark Edwards in Seattle, Washington from Pasadena, California. The young man has signed this card "Lewis".

13

Motorcycling Through History

Indian motorcycles were hugely popular in the first part of the last century. This page shows a few more examples. By 1913 production had reached a record 32,000 machines. At right is most likely a 1913 model, single cylinder, 4 H.P.. Machine. The license plate indicates that the cycle was registered in Oregon, in 1914.

Indian

Like the cycle above, this one was also registered in Oregon, in 1914. The rather stern looking gentleman shown here is probably riding a 1914 seven H.P., two speed regular model.

This is another really nice photo of an Indian from the same era as those above. This one is most likely a 1913, twin cylinder.

"The Twin's the Thing!"

The 1913 *Indian* Motocycle

7 H.P. Twin Cylinder has the reserve power that carries you at any pace over any road. Through deep mud and sand and up steep, rough hills. Wonderfully smooth running motor. Another important and unique comfort feature of the 1913 Indian is the equipment of foot-boards in addition to pedals. The latter are in reality fitted only for the purpose of starting the motor, similar to cranking an automobile. Once started, the rider has the choice of two comfortable riding positions with the double brake action and absolute control assured in each instance.

A free Demonstration from any of our 2000 dealers throughout the country Write for free 1913 literature describing all models and improvements

Prices { 4 H.P. Single, $200
7 H.P. Twin, $250 } f. o. b. Factory

THE HENDEE MFG. CO., 953 State St., SPRINGFIELD, MASS.

Branches and Service Stations:
Chicago   Denver   San Francisco   Toronto   Atlanta   London

14

Chapter I: American Cycles

POST CARD

1910 was the first year that Indian introduced it's loop frame, discarding the diamond shape of previous years. This is probably an early 1910 model. Later in the model year the famous Indian script appeared on some machines. This single cylinder engine had a displacement of 316 cc and was rated at 5 H.P. mph. All this for only $ 215.00

POST CARD
THIS SIDE FOR THE ADDRESS

The Indian shown here is a very early model. It is most likely a 1902 or 1903 model. Lack of spring cushion fork makes it pre-1905. No chain cover puts it before 1904. This machine has a double size aftermarket battery box and a handlebar horn, as well as a tool pouch on the saddle. The earliest Indians had engines supplied by the Aurora Automatic Machine Company, later to build their own machine under the Thor name. The early engines were 213 cc with 1.75 H.P. Finding these very early Indian photo's is rare.

Seen here is what appears to be a photo from a showroom floor with a variety of cycles on display. Foremost is the Ca. 1917 Powerplus Indian with sidecar that dominates the photo. The rounded gas tank was new for 1917 replacing the sectioned, hand built tanks of previous years. The cradle spring frame is clearly seen on this example. In 1917 Indian entered the war as a major supplier of cycles to the military.

Motorcycling Through History

The three real photo's on this page are all of early Indians. At right is a card that has a divided back and was posted in 1911 to Berkeley, California. In referring to the gentleman in the photo, Alice, the writer asks *"Would anybody think this piece of humanity could go 90 mile a minute or is it an hour?"* In fact, a ca. 1910-1911, 1000 cc Indian twin set up for racing had a top speed of 100 MPH.

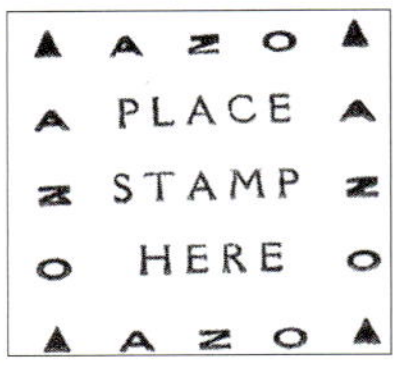

Shown here is a unique photo that is probably staged. The man on the right appears to be holding broken pieces of the bike, but the machine appears to be intact. This is probably a 1912 model lacking the rear leaf suspension and incorporating a forward hand crank mechanism which was introduced on 1912 TT models. These gentlemen appear to be just a bit too happy after a crash.

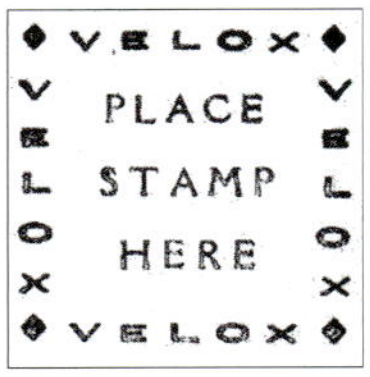

This superbly detailed and clear photo has Roseburg, Oregon written on the back. The Indian pictured is probably a 1914 model. Sharp side view images like this one are especially desirable and collectible.

16

Chapter I: American Cycles

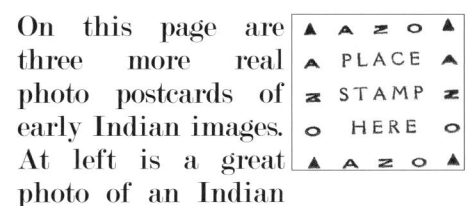

On this page are three more real photo postcards of early Indian images. At left is a great photo of an Indian motorcycle riding club. There was always intense brand loyalty between Indian and Harley riders, just as there is today among owners of specific marques. In this photo one lone Harley rider stands out at the far left wearing his Harley-Davidson shirt. His broad smile shows no indication that he is unaccepted.

In this photo are perhaps a brother and sister sitting on an early Indian of ca. 1913 vintage. Handwriting on the card says *"Kansas City, ca. 1921"*. This Indian still had a left hand shifter that moved to the right side in later years. Noticeable also in this photo is that the foot pedals have been removed. This was generally done by the owner in an effort to customize or streamline the machine. The large battery box under the seat seems distinctive for this model.

This lovely lady with her nice corsage sits on her early teens Indian. This model is earlier than the one above because it lacks the rear leaf spring suspension that was introduced in 1913. This could be a 1912 model. This photo appears to have been taken for some special occasion. Perhaps this is a mother and daughter in their loveliest of dresses which do not make for good riding attire.

17

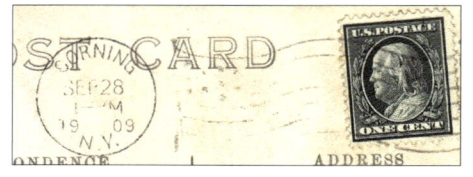

Motorcycling Through History

The last twenty years has seen a tremendous growth in the number of women riding motorcycles. Their grandmothers set the example by breaking down another male barrier. The very feminine looking woman shown here is standing beside her unidentified motorcycle. This card was posted at Corning N.Y on Sept. 28, 1909.

"*Try this on your Harley Daveson*" says the caption on this card". Ok, there has to be a show off in every crowd and as everyone knows, Harley riders like to stand out in a crowd. Back in 1916 when this fellow was performing his stunt, the Harley Davidson-Company was building it's 16J model of which this is an example. The rounded fuel tank sets this one apart from earlier machines.

These two young ladies obviously do not mind having their photo taken astride such a great motorcycle. The Indian shown appears to be a 1914, 7 HP, two speed model. The tank mounted tool box was introduced in that year. Electric lights were also available in that year although this example still uses an acetylene gas light. A note on this card says "Falls Creek, PA".

18

Chapter I: American Cycles

The Harley-Davidson Motorcycle was the creation of William Harley and Arthur and Walter Davidson. In 1903 the first of their machines was born. It was not until around 1910-1911 that production began to increase substantially. The model at left is probably a 1910 model 6. Unfortunately nothing is know of the individual riding the motorcycle. Early Harley cards like this one are especially rare and valuable.

This well dressed individual seems proud to show off his Ca. 1914 Harley twin. This 811 cc motorcycle had a top speed of 65 mph. and cost less than $300.00 when new. The round cylinder atop the gas tank contained the acetylene gas to fuel the headlight.

HARLEY-DAVIDSON

Flying the American flag, Mr. F. S.L. is decked out in the finest riding apparel. This is a 1917 "F-Head" twin. 1917 saw a change in paint from the former gray color to an olive green as a sign of patriotism for the war in Europe. Harley-Davidson was rapidly becoming the largest American manufacturer of motorcycles, a title they claimed in 1918.

19

Motorcycling Through History

Although the clarity of this picture is not terrific, the image itself is really interesting. Taken ca. 1912, based on the age of the motorcycles, this scene appears to be set in one of the plain's states. On the left is a Harley-Davidson and on the right is an Indian.

"We should Worry!"

So reads the penned in caption on this photo. What is interesting is guessing whether the author really meant to use an exclamation mark or would a question mark be more fitting. These fashion conscious young men are sitting on an early teens Harley-Davidson.

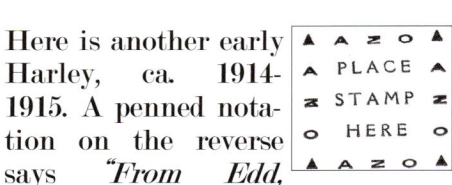

Here is another early Harley, ca. 1914-1915. A penned notation on the reverse says *"From Edd, 1915".* The chain, final drive on this machine dates it from 1914 or later. This machine is equipped with a rear passenger seat and canvas rear wheel covering. The roads in rural America at that time were terrible and could become nearly impassable if weather conditions deteriorated. Protection for the rider and passenger was highly desirable.

Chapter I: American Cycles

"Lets go!, Easter Walters, movie star of the Pathe Film Co." Easter is sitting on a 1919-1923 Harley-Davidson, Sport model. It is unique because of the 35.6 cu. in. horizontally opposed, fore and aft, twin engine. Easter is credited for acting in "The Tigers Trail" and "Common Clay", both from 1919. This is an uncommon postcard.

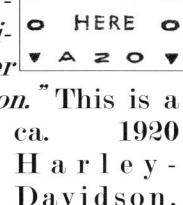

"Gertrude Hoffman, Favorite of the Orpheum Theatre Circuit, leaving the Chicago store with her new Harley-Davidson." This is a ca. 1920 Harley-Davidson, 61 cu. in. V-twin.

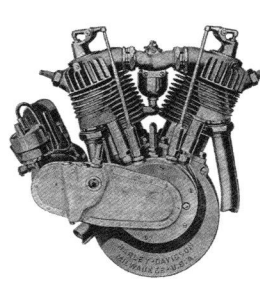

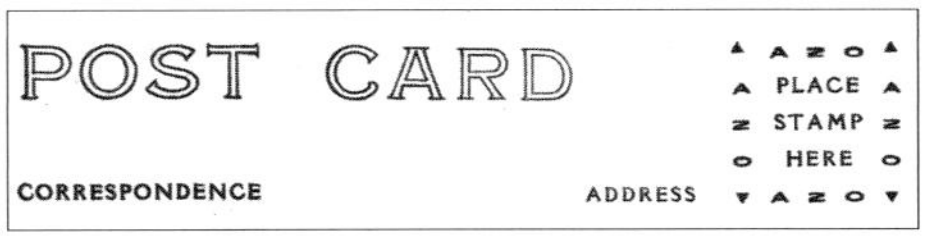

"Gertrude Hoffman, popular artist of the Orpheum Theatre Circuit, in her Harley-Davidson."

This card is another view of the same sidecar rig shown above. These cards of Ms. Hoffman are fairly uncommon and quite desirable to collectors of both motorcycle and movie star memorabilia.

21

Motorcycling Through History

POST CARD

On this page are various views of Alfred LeRoy as he pursued his goal of traveling the U.S. by motorcycle.

"*Legless one-arm driver now on 50,000 mile tour of the United States. Machine constructed and furnished by Mr. Barney Oldfield, world-famous auto speed king.*" Card printed by Geo. Rice & Sons printers, Los Angeles.

Post Card

In 1915 Electric lights were added to the Harley-Davidson which can be seen in the photo's at right and below. Perhaps the acetylene lamp shown in the above photo was later upgraded to the better lighting. "*Legless one-arm driver now on 50,000 mile tour of the United States. Total mileage traveled up to August 20th, 1918 24,316. On fifth trip across the North American Continent using Harley-Davidson motorcycle and sidecar. Don't forget the fourth liberty loan.*"

Post Card

Mr. LeRoy is riding a 1916 J-series Harley twin. With this model the gas tank took on a more rounded look as opposed to the square cut corners of the previous models.

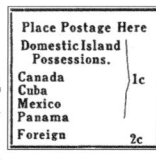

"*Legless one-arm driver on tour U.S.A. Total mileage covered up to July 4th, 1919, 51,117 using Harley-Davidson motorcycle and sidecar.*" This series of cards is not uncommon.

Chapter I: American Cycles

POST CARD

PLACE STAMP HERE

"In a fall of 1,800 feet from a balloon, Mr. New lost the sight of one eye, broke his back in two places and crushed his feet and legs so badly, that both legs had to be amputated. He is now on a 100,000 mile trip— his motorcycle covering the worst trails in the country. Goodrich Tires, which he uses exclusively, have kept his trip clear from tire troubles and the worries that often beset the most able-bodied of tourists."

Price, What You Care to Pay

POST CARD

PLACE A STAMP HERE

"Mr. Coogan, operating a motorcycle despite the loss of the use of both legs. Down but not out, just trying to make good. He is now on a 100,000 mile trip. His motorcycle covering the worst trails in the country." As seen in this group of cards, Harley-Davidson was the choice for disabled riders. This card and the one above show up occasionally on auction sites.

There is small printing on the top of the sidecar that this man is riding in. It says: *"John A. Sebastian, San Francisco, CA."* In the window behind him is the word "Motorcycle". This card was published by the Pacific Novelty Co. San Francisco. This is another late teens Harley-Davidson with a wonderful passenger vehicle specially equipped for Mr. Sebastian. This postcard is quite rare.

23

Motorcycling Through History

What a great image this is. Dated to 1914 by the Indiana license plate on the Harley-Davidson, the composition of individuals is most interesting. One gentleman is reading a current "Wild West" paper while grandpa is posed with his squeeze box. This could very well be a three generation photo with the youngest being the rider of the Harley. Any collector would love to have this card.

Riding her Flanders 4 motorcycle, Miss "Cy." Woodman has apparently made a cross country excursion. This would have been anything but an easy ride in 1911 or 1912 when she made the trip based on the model of Flanders she is on. This 4 H.P. machine was built in Detroit, Michigan and had a top speed of 45 mph. This is quite a rare card. In general Flanders cards are hard to find.

This lovely lady is standing beside her 269 cc, single cylinder Excelsior. This is a seldom seen model being one of the smallest in the Excelsior lineup. It was introduced in 1914 to compete with the Triumph "Baby" which was a 225 cc model built from 1914-1925. Most images of early Excelsior machines are of the larger more powerful ones. The license plate on this photo says 1917.

24

Chapter I: American Cycles

All of the cards on this page show examples of Excelsior Motorcycles. Excelsior cards are very common and easy to find. The one below shows a young lady out on her ca. 1914 sidecar rig.

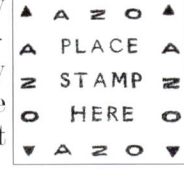

This well dressed man in his checkered cap is riding a somewhat newer model of Excelsior than the others on this page. This one probably dates from around 1919.

The image at left is especially sharp providing nice detail. This may be a 1912 Excelsior.

25

Motorcycling Through History

This postcard shows Curtis Wright on his ca. 1908-1910 Excelsior, belt drive single. The 500 cc engine was more than adequate to compete in racing. It is obvious that the cycle in this photo has been modified for the race track. With fenders removed and the low swept handle bars, Mr. Wright appears ready for all challengers. Cards with a racing theme are highly sought after.

In 1911 the Excelsior Supply Co. which began building motorcycles in 1906, sold out to Arnold-Schwinn and Co. of Chicago, the bicycle manufacturer. In 1912 the single cylinder engine was dropped in favor of the popular V-twin. With the acquisition of the company by Schwinn, the name was changed to the Excelsior Motor Manufacturing and Supply Company.

This real photo postcard was addressed to Miss Anna Larson from Esther Wenz. The Excelsior is a pre-1912 model. The attractive tank decal depicts the company name and within the large X are the words "Excelsior Auto Cycle." Paved roads were not available at the time this photo was taken. It is doubtful that white dresses would have stayed white. Was one of the ladies the proud owner of this machine? The early cards that feature women are highly collectible.

Chapter I: American Cycles

the Minneapolis

The license plate on this cycle says Iowa 1911. It is nice to have that bit of information to go along with the identification. In this case the machine is a Minneapolis. The cycles were built in Minnesota from about 1908 until 1915 and had engines supplied by Thiem, Thor, and Spacke as well as their own single cylinder, side valve design which this cycle appears to have.

DAYTON

Dayton motorcycles were made at Dayton, Ohio by the Davis Sewing Machine Co. In terms of a company diversifying, this seems quite an odd pairing of products. The cycle shown here is possibly a 1913 model. The company built these machines from 1911-1917 using Spacke V-twin engines.

The card at left has an especially sharp image of two new Excelsior machines. The man in the photo is probably posing for a friend who owns the other machine. It is interesting to note that after the demise of this famous motorcycle in 1931, it was reborn in 1999 with the Excelsior-Henderson name. A product of the Hanlon brothers of Minnesota, the company received a lot of initial fanfare but failed financially.

27

Motorcycling Through History

This gentleman is sitting on his Ca. 1919 Excelsior twin which was made in Chicago.

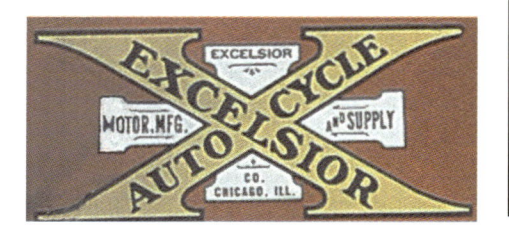

Henderson motorcycles came on the scene in 1912 with the introduction of a four cylinder model. It had nearly a 1000 cc displacement in a frame that was stretched to a 65" wheelbase. The cycle shown here may be a 1915 model. The Henderson Brothers ran the company until absorbed by Ignaz Schwinn who built bicycles and owned the Excelsior Motor Mfg. Co. Any card showing a Henderson is rare and valuable.

Thiem motorcycles were made at St. Paul Minnesota. The company lasted from 1900 until 1913 and produced proprietary engines as well as it's own complete machines, like the one shown here. Typically the engines were 500 cc side valve singles. The company also built the Cyclone motorcycle. This is a rare image of a great early American motorcycle.

28

Chapter I: American Cycles

This cycle started out as a Waverly as early as 1909. The engines were sold as Waverly and Mack for other manufacturers. The Waverly motorcycle became, for a short time the P.E.M. using a single cylinder engine. In 1912 a V twin was renamed the Jefferson after Jefferson, Wisconsin where it was made.

Here is an image of an extremely rare motorcycle. It is a Greyhound, built from 1907-1914 at Aurora, Illinois. Until 1910 it used the Thor engine and after that, engines by E.R. Thomas and Auto-Bi. This machine is probably post 1910.

Excelsior motorcycles were especially popular from their beginnings in 1908 until their demise in 1931. The one pictured here is probably from ca. 1918-1919. Unique in this example are the full wheel covers which were occasionally seen on Indians and other machines of the time. After WWI, Excelsior resumed production of motorcycles for civilian use. This could very well be one of those after war models. The ladies and children are nicely posed.

29

Motorcycling Through History

The Emblem motorcycle was built at Angola N.Y. between 1907 and 1925. This example is probably from about 1912-1913 and appears to be a V-twin.

Shown below is a Real photo postcard of a ca. 1908 M & M Motorcycle. Nice views of this model and other M & M cycles are shown in the chapter on advertising.

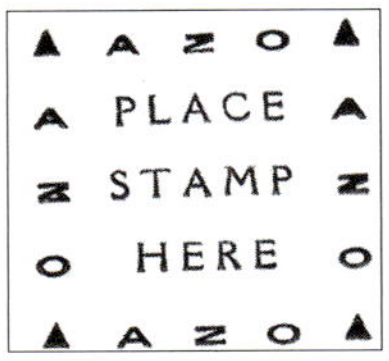

The strange looking device shown here is a Smith Motor Wheel. The attachment allowed bicyclists to move along at up to 30 mph with a 197 cc engine attached to the rear of the bike. These engines were made by the A.O. Smith Co. at Milwaukee, Wisconsin between 1914 and 1924. This was a common attachment in the last century, but the image is very hard to find.

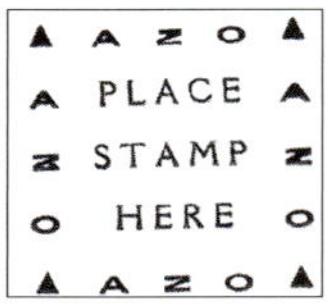

30

Chapter I: American Cycles

The Yale motorcycle was built at Toledo, Ohio between 1902 and 1915 by the Consolidated Manufacturing Company. Prior to 1910 machines produced there were know as the Yale-California a product of the California Motorcycle Co. that was purchased by Consolidated. This single cylinder model was probably made in 1910.

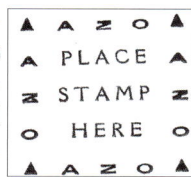

This card dates from the pre-teens of the last century. The photo of these boys interspersed with the tranquil setting depicted in the front design is quite unique. They are riding a ca. 1910 Yale cycle like the one shown above.

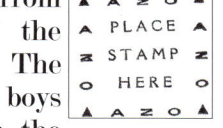

The simplicity of the plain divided back on this card is in sharp contrast to the wonderful image on the front. Generally cards of this era were sepia toned whereas this one is uniquely blue. In the foreground is a very early Curtiss single and behind it is one of Indian's very early machines. Both of these machines could be from before 1905. Looking closely, the camel hump tank of the Indian is seen.

31

Motorcycling Through History

Shown below is a superb example of a hand tinted photograph. It shows a ca. 1912-1913 Pope. Popes were built between 1911 & 1918 at Hartford, CT and Westfield, MA. Unique in this photo is the side seat arrangement which was a popular accessory of the time. This is an extremely rare and valuable postcard.

Before there were motorcycles, bicycles ruled. One of the premier manufacturers of bicycles and tricycles was the Pope Mfg. Co. In the 1870s this company was producing a variety of two and three wheel, pedal powered transports. The Columbia bicycle was one of many private label bikes that Pope built for others. This advertising card proclaims the merits and quality of the Columbia bicycle. The back of the card continues with testimonials.

Seen here is another example of a Pope motorcycle. This is a ca. 1911-1912 Mo. H. Pope single. The Pope name was derived from the founder of the company. He was a Civil War, Lieutenant Colonel (Union Army) by the name of Albert Agustus Pope. In the late 1800s he was building bicycles and automobiles and later became a major supplier of motorcycles which he supplied under private label to other companies.

32

Chapter I: American Cycles

The Aurora Automatic Machinery Co. began building motorcycle engines in 1902. They were under contract to Indian until 1907 when they began building their own machines. Shown is one of the early Thor singles from about 1913. It was either a 4 or 5 H.P. Machine. Many Thor motorcycles were produced over a long period of time and their images are fairly common.

The lovely lady in this photo is sitting in her wicker sidecar, which like the cycle was made by Thor. The Thor logo is visible on the front side of the passenger foot rest. This rig dates from 1909-1910. The four link-fork was moved from it's lower position to this position in 1909. This particular postcard image is quite rare.

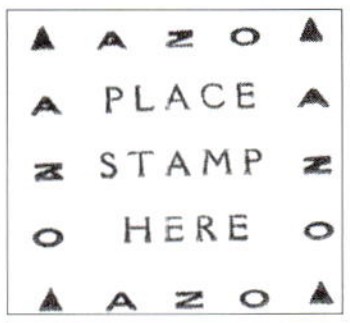

Here is another great image of an early Thor machine. Like the one above, it dates from 1909 or later. Thor engines and machines were built at Aurora, Illinois from 1902 until 1917. The company became prominent in racing and participated well against both Indian and Harley-Davidson.

33

Motorcycling Through History

What a wonderful family picture this is. Here is dad with his two daughters and even the dog along for the ride. The photo was taken at Savannah, Missouri on Sept. 16, 1910. Shown are Dr. J.J. Spencer with his daughters, Mary Ceoline, 4 years old, and Nellie Eizabeth, 2 years, six months old. The card was posted to friends in Greencastle MO. On Sept. 26, 1910.

The Aurora Automatic Machine Co. began building motorcycle engines in 1902 as a supplier to Indian and others. In 1907 the company began building their own motorcycles under the Thor name. It is hard to say what this brand of motorcycle is, because most distinguishing features are covered by the people. It does appear that the engine could very well be a Thor twin. which was built at Aurora, Illinois up until 1917.

Here is a wonderful example of a very early Thor motorcycle. It's engine design and placement are noticeably similar to the earliest Indians. As the original supplier of engines to Indian, Thor ultimately went their own direction as did Indian. The lower four link fork assembly identifies this machine as pre-1909. It may be one of the first designs after the 1907 introduction.

Chapter I: American Cycles

The Wagner motorcycle was built at St. Paul, Minnesota between the years 1901 & 1914. Three examples are shown on this page. The one at left is probably the earliest example. It is believed to be pre-1909. Wagner postcards are desirable and uncommon.

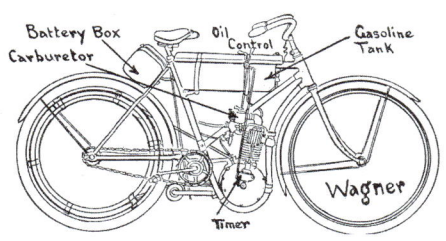

Seen here is another Wagner. This appears to be a ca. 1909 model. The four sided battery box located behind the saddle on the model shown above later changed to a three sided box situated under the saddle as shown here. Notice the saddle height. It looks as though this rider would not even be able to reach the ground with his feet, once on the machine.

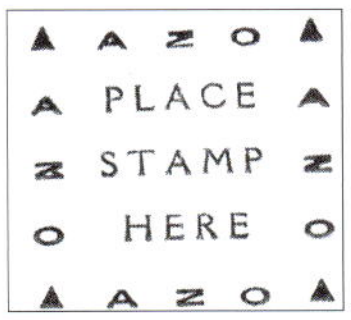

At left is another divided back, AZO card that dates from about 1911. Without a powerful loupe it is not possible to see the date printed on the side of the gas tank, but it reads 4-1911 and looks like the one shown below.

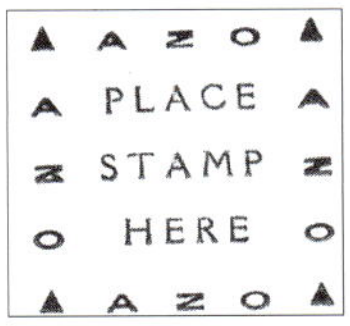

Wagner '4'-'1911'

35

Motorcycling Through History

Glenn H. Curtiss was one of the great aviation pioneers. He has also secured a place in history with his V8 motorcycle which he rode to a record 136 MPH in 1907. He was actually testing the engine prior to installing it in an airplane. His mile run in 26-2/5 seconds was a world's record. This is a plain divided back card "Made by H.M. Benner, Hammondsport N.Y." This is a fairly common card.

This color version of the above card is quite rare and was Made in Germany and published by James H. Smellye, Chemist & Druggist, Hammondsport, N.Y.. It is shown to be card No. C7483. It was posted on March 20, 1908 from Buffalo, N.Y. and received at New Haven Conn. On March 22nd. The front text reads: "*World's Record-Ormond Beach, Fla. 1 mile - 26 2/5 seconds. 8 cylinder, 40 H.P. motor cycle, built by the Curtiss Manufacturing Company, Hammondsport N.Y.*"

Seen here is a fine example of an early Yale twin cylinder machine. It probably dates from 1912. A year later the company made some styling changes including the shape of the gas tank and a new logo. Although it is mostly missing on this machine, the logo would have read as shown below.

YALE 4P

36

Chapter I: American Cycles

This card is as interesting for the image as the text on the front. It reads: *"C.B. Tainey on a Yale motorcycle which made 4,600 miles on all kinds of country roads. Won fst. in the 5 mi. race on a 1/2 mile track at the Brookings Co. Fair in 7 min. 14 sec. Sep. 23, 1910."* Mr. Tainey is shown under the X in this picture.

At left are two young men preparing to ride their Reading Standard cycle. This cycle appears to be from about 1911. The Reading Standard Co. was founded in 1903 and continued production until 1922. The company was located in Pennsylvania and produced single and twin cylinder machines. Engine sizes ranged from the 557 cc single to an 1180 cc twin.

Here is an example of an early Michaelson motorcycle. These machines were produced by the same company that made the Minneapolis in the city of the same name. They were made from 1908-1914. The example shown here is licensed in Washington for 1916, but the cycle is certainly earlier. The card is very uncommon.

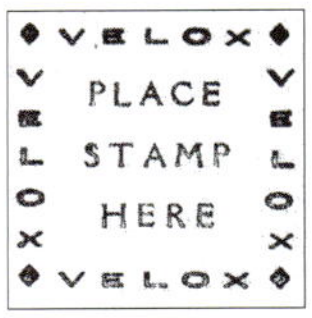

Motorcycling Through History

The Pierce Cycle Co. of Buffalo, N.Y. was a pioneer in American motorcycling. They were the first American company to build a four cylinder engine, influenced by the FN of Belgium. The Pierce line of cycles were built between 1909 and 1913. Shown here is Mr. Harry Henley in a photo taken ca. 1911 at Richmond, IN. The large frame tubes on this machine were used to carry gasoline and oil. Cards showing the Pierce motorcycle are not easy to find.

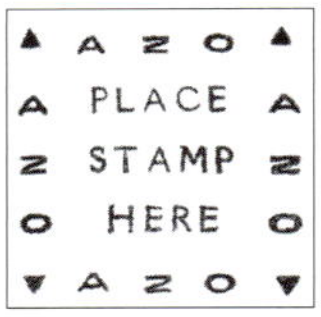

At right is a picture of Mr. R.L. Clark, and his 1910 Pierce 4 cylinder. Mr. Clark was a prominent motorcycle dealer selling Reading Standards and Indians at his shop in Milwaukee. This photo was probably taken in 1910 just prior to a trip he was making to or from Chicago. On his handlebar is a banner that says Chicago. The Pierce was a great motorcycle, but unfortunately cost more to produce than it could be sold for, thus it's short life.

Pierce also made single cylinder models of it's motorcycle. They were probably only made in 1912 and 1913. It is not know what the occasion was that prompted the nice family portrait here, but the young lady on the motorcycle seems especially happy.

PIERCE

38

Chapter I: American Cycles

For this gentleman, the dog is man's best friend, unless of course it's his two Cleveland motorcycles. These machines ca. 1918 were made at Cleveland, Ohio. They were light weight (150 lbs.) and cost about a dollar a pound ($150.00). They had a two stroke, 220 cc engine that put out 3.5 H.P.. They were built in Ohio from 1915 until 1929.

Cleveland

The young lady shown here is sitting comfortably upon a ca. 1910 Flying Merkel. Between 1902 and 1915 when it was produced, the Merkel gained a good reputation and performed well on racing circuits. Designed by Joseph Merkel, the machines were built at a succession of locations including, Milwaukee, WI, Pottstown, PA., and Middletown, Ohio. This is an uncommon card.

THE FLYING MERKEL

One of the great names in aviation and motorcycle history was Glenn Curtiss. His machines were built at Hammondsport, New York from 1901-1913. The V-twin shown here could be from around 1910. It had a displacement of 1000 cc putting out 5-6 horsepower. Glenn rode his V-twin to a record breaking 76 mph in 1907 and then brought out his V-8 machine which reached 136.36 mph. Any postcard image of the Curtiss motorcycle is highly desirable and sought after.

Motorcycling Through History

Standing beside "The Real J. Wesley, Sewing Machine shop" are these men who stand at the crossroads of old versus new technology. The bicycle rider on the left and the motorcycle rider on the right. The cycle is probably an Indian of 1905 vintage. This was the first year the Indian incorporated the cartridge-spring front suspension, an improvement over it's bone shaking predecessors.

This ca. 1914 Harley twin sits beside other examples of modern automotive engineering. These vehicles are loaded with farm animals which appear to be sheep. This is a nice historical look at early transportation.

Seen here is probably a 1908 Thor, single cylinder model. Earlier models like the one shown on page 34 had the engine incorporated into the rear frame down tube, as did the earliest Indians. This would-be racing enthusiast may have in fact competed in early competitions. His machine has little added weight and the rear stand has been removed. Again, because it has a racing theme, this card is quite desirable.

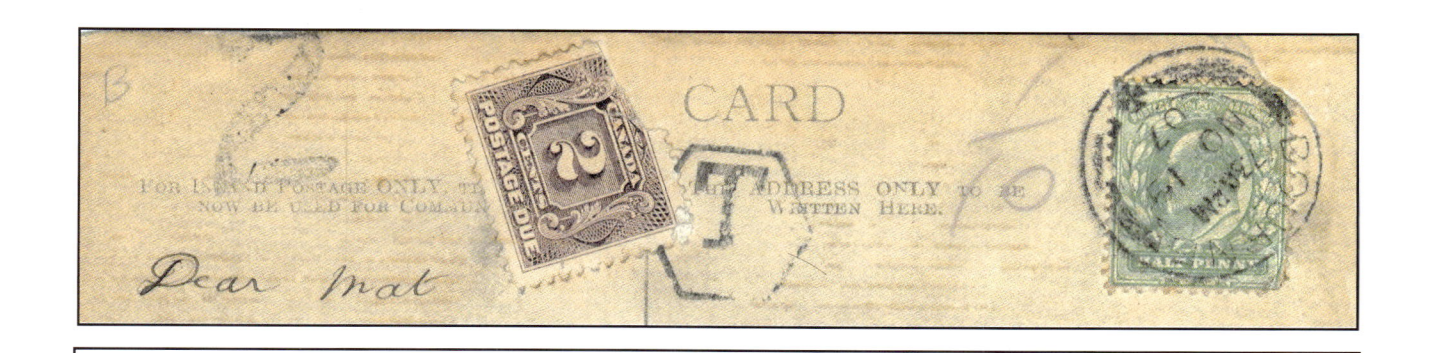

CHAPTER II: EUROPEAN MOTORCYCLES

Motorcycling Through History

BREV-KORT

This image may be of a German cycle which has similarities to the Komet built in Germany between 1902 and 1905. The Komet Co. was originally a bicycle factory.

The image here shows a DeDion or similar design tricycle built in France beginning in 1895. The De Dion-Bouton design was widely copied because of it's great success. This French card was posted in June, 1901 to Luneville, France.

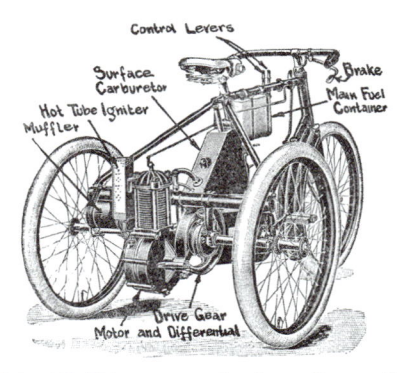

This idyllic scene is found on the front of a French card which appears to have been posted in June of 1900. It shows a De Dion style tricycle pulling a passenger trailer. The river scene is a view of the park at Anvers (Antwerp).

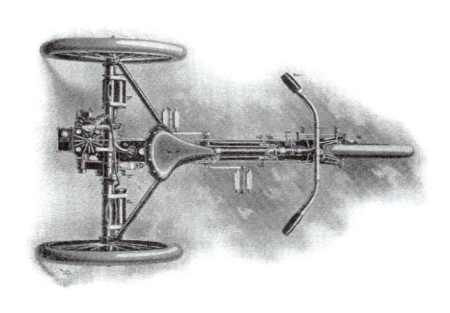

42

Chapter II: European Cycles

In the foreground of this picture is an 1885 De Dion Bouton tricycle which was on display at the 1914 Exposition International in Lyon France. This steam driven machine was the precursor of the internal combustion engine that Comte Albert de Dion introduced in a machine of 1889 that was widely copied. This is an extremely rare card.

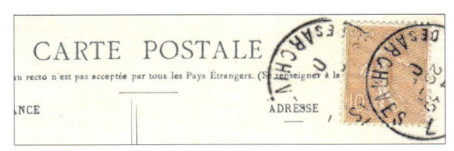

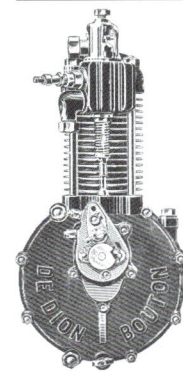

Apparently repairs are being made on this De Dion tricycle. *"Une Panne on Tricycle"* reads the caption. The photographer and his mark are shown here.

Cliché F. Gébert

Shown here is a quadricycle from the turn of the last century, possibly a Porteous Butler from 1898.

"*The rattletrap and the legless cripple. The automobile revs up it's engine breaking the eardrums, and the driver re-inflates his tires. He has time and then finally his wife from behind a bush, without hurrying, proclaims to him: let the vagrant dash by*".

43

Motorcycling Through History

A little known motorcycle is shown here. It is an Orionette, which was made in Germany between 1921 and 1925. This company mostly produced 129 cc— 148 cc two stroke machines. The only identifying information on this very plain divided back card is the number, A 162. With the gauntlet gloves and exceptionally tall riding boots, this rider is well prepared for the cold that he must be feeling. In general, motorcycle riders know the true meaning of cold.

This divided back card does not bear a stamp or any other identifying information. It carries a written message and the date, July 1911. Shown here is a superb example of an FN cycle that was built in Belgium. Introduced in 1904 and built until 1957, the FN was revolutionary for it's inline four cylinder engine and shaft drive. Clear and detailed images of the FN cycle as shown here are very hard to find.

Wanderer motorcycles were built in Germany between 1902 and 1929. They ultimately sold out to Jawa which was a relatively new company at that time. The Wanderer machines were good, reliable motorcycles with single cylinder and V-twin configurations. Many of these machines were used by the Germans during WWI. This postcard has a divided back with no information. It probably dates from the late teens. Images of Wanderer motorcycles are not found too often.

44

Chapter II: European Cycles

Incredible is the only way to describe the clarity and content of this photo. This picture may be from as early as 1906 and shows a variety of Rex cycles. These machines were built in Coventry, England between 1900 and 1933. Varieties of engines were used including Werner, Blackburne and later on the JAP and Villagers. This is a valuable and rare postcard.

Some of the more obscure motorcycles become a challenge to identify as is the case here. There are no reference books that depict every model of every manufacturer. At times it becomes a matter of just looking at similarities. One assumption that is likely, is that this is a German motorcycle. The shape of the gas tank on this model is not common nor are the dual down tubes of the front fork assembly. More research will have to be done on this machine.

CARTE POSTALE

Motobecane and Motoconfort were produced in France by the same company. Models were often identical and generally speaking were small displacement machines although 500cc and 750cc machines were built in the 1930s. The company began production in 1922. The model shown in this picture may be as early as 1923.

Motobecane

The NSU Motorcycle Co. was founded in Germany and operated between 1901 and 1958. The gentleman riding the model shown here is known to be Franz Goldman of Plainfield N.J. He was a worker at the St. Louis Worlds Fair in 1903 but it is unknown when this picture was taken. The NSU shown may date from around 1915. Images of NSU motorcycles are fairly common on postcards.

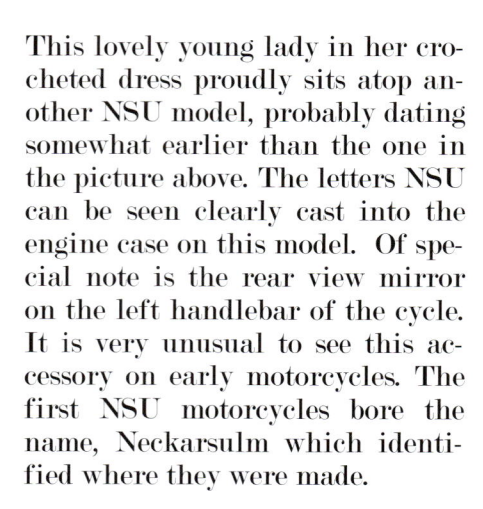

This lovely young lady in her crocheted dress proudly sits atop another NSU model, probably dating somewhat earlier than the one in the picture above. The letters NSU can be seen clearly cast into the engine case on this model. Of special note is the rear view mirror on the left handlebar of the cycle. It is very unusual to see this accessory on early motorcycles. The first NSU motorcycles bore the name, Neckarsulm which identified where they were made.

This distinctly European card caries an image of a ca. 1914 NSU. This is a particularly sharp photo that appears to be Swiss/German. The sign above the door of the establishment says *"Pub of Rossli."* With a high power loupe, the NSU can be read on the side of the gas tank. The belt drives on these early machines were always a cause of concern when no guards were in place.

Chapter II, European Cycles

Pictured here is a Lincoln-Elk motorcycle. It was made at Lincoln, England between 1902 and about 1926. This example is a very early one. The card is postmarked Nov. 19, 1907. It was sent from England to Vancouver B.C. Canada. The passenger trailer is a superb example of the best wicker work of the day.

Here is a very happy looking family out for a ride in their single cylinder, 2 H.P. Leon-Bollee tricycle. This card probably dates from around 1900 although no date is available. These tricycles were built at Le Mans France beginning in 1896. There is nothing to indicate where this photo was taken. The handle at the left elbow of the driver is the gear control and belt tensioning lever. The finned cylinder can be clearly seen ahead of the carburetor and silencer.

"*Love and best wishes to you all*" the card says. It is addressed to Miss Cooper in Newtown Tasmania and was mailed from New South Wales on Dec. 5th, year illegible. No doubt the man posing with his cycle is the author of the card.

Motorcycling Through History

This card and the one directly below are of the same individual. Each card has a divided back with no information at all about the origins of the pictures. The gentleman was kind enough to give us both right and left side views of his motorcycle.

JAMES

The James motorcycle was built at Birmingham, England between 1902 and 1964. Originally founded in 1870 by Harold James, the company did not produce a motorcycle until 1902 and after Harold's death. Many styles and sizes of motorcycles were built by this company and they produced large quantities for the military in WWI, particularly for the Belgians and Russians. The cycle in these photo's may be as early as 1914 or into the early 1920s.

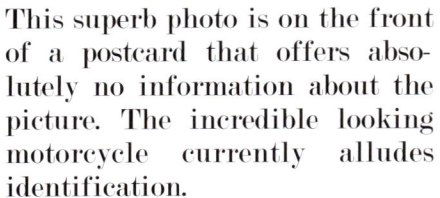

This superb photo is on the front of a postcard that offers absolutely no information about the picture. The incredible looking motorcycle currently alludes identification.

Chapter II: European Cycles

The card at left is where it all began for me. This studio image on a simple divided back card was the first motorcycle postcard that I purchased. I found it at an antique show in England where my collecting passion for this type of material was born. The cycle is an early teens Triumph, but the photo could have been taken later. The card was not posted or written on and there is no indication of who the photographer may have been.

Sitting happily on her "Panther" motorcycle, this young lady certainly seems ready to get off the center stand and be on her way. The Panther was built in Yorkshire, England by the originators of the P & M cycle, Jonah Phelon and Richard Moore. Panther (P & M) machines were built from 1900-1965. This model probably dates from the 1930s.

At left is an image of a motorcycle that I have not identified. Barely visible on the gas tank is what is left of the letter "R". This card says only, *"Yours Sincerely, Jack."* This is probably a British cycle from the twenties or thirties. My closest guess was Raleigh.

49

Motorcycling Through History

Birmingham England was the home of the Levis Motor Works. Begun in 1906 by the brothers William and Arthur Hughes Butterfield, Levis motorcycles first became a reality in 1911. The name was chosen from the Latin phrase, "Levis et Celer" which means "Light and Quick". The model shown here is probably from about 1920. Except for the up-sweeping front fender, this example looks exactly like a 1921, 211cc Levis Popular which often was referred to simply as the "Pop".

These two ladies appear very comfortable astride an English made, single cylinder Zenith Gradua, with JAP engine. These machines were built in England between 1904 and 1950. A number of manufacturers engines were used from horizontal twins, to V-twins and singles. The model here dates from ca. 1920. The photo was taken on Madiera Dr. Brighton, England

Here we see a well attired lady on her BSA single. This machine is a side valve single dating from the early 1920s. Built in Birmingham England by a company historically founded in the gun trade, the BSA motorcycle first appeared in 1910. BSA are the initials which stand for Birmingham Small Arms Co. founded in 1861 to build bicycles.

50

Chapter II European Cycles

POST CARD
Correspondence. *Address.*

Triumph has always been one of the world's great motorcycles. From 1903 until the present day it continues to thrill riders. This is probably a pre-1913 model that had a 499cc engine and could reach 46 mph.

A pencil notation on the back of this card says: Triumph, 1910, but that is open for debate. This handsome gentleman, believed to be the brother of Ebenezer Scrooge, looks as though he has seen happier days. His memory has been preserved in this remarkably sharp photo. The card was never posted and has a plain divided back.

CARTE POSTALE

Here is a WWI era soldier sitting astride his ca. 1915 Triumph. At least 30,000 of these machines were built for the military. They were the 550cc, model H.

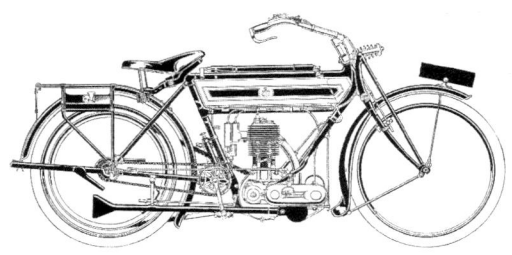

Motorcycling Through History

This photo shows two classic European motorcycles. In front is a BSA and behind it an FN. The BSA dates from the early to mid 1920s and the FN is probably the same. The following date is written on the back of the card:

Gekregen 29 Jan 1928.

An ink stamp says:

THE EXTREME RADIO FOTO
Ged. Neuwesloot, ALKMAAR
HELDER, 22 JAN. 1928 (N. Holland, 20 mi. NNW of Amsterdam)

In period costume these two Dutch ladies better hope that they do not catch a strong head wind. The caption at the bottom of the photo reads: *"A Holland farmer and her friend"*. What is most interesting is that this photo and the one below are the same cycle and location. In all likelihood these are family portraits with the head of the family shown below.

Nadruk verboden. No. 9.
Uitgave: Firma A. v. Loo & Co.
Yerseke

Eysink began building motorcycles in the Netherlands in 1901 and continued until 1956. This example is probably from the teens, but the card is no help in proving that. The center dividing line of the card identifies the publisher. It says: Uitgave: Firma A. van Loo & Co., Yerseke. In addition, one other printing on the card says: Nadruk verbodel. This is an especially nice photo of an early and uncommon motorcycle. Having both this card and the one above are an unusual find.

52

Chapter II: European Cycles

Each card on this page has a plain divided back and was not posted. No information is provided on any of the cards. To the left is a nice close up view of a Douglas motorcycle. The model shown probably dates from around 1914. These opposed, twin cylinder machines saw a lot of use by the British military in WWI. After the war, Douglas became heavily involved in building machines for dirt track racing.

The studio photo shown at left depicts another of those motorcycles that I have not positively identified. The large outside flywheel was characteristic of a variety of machines including Premier, Douglas, early Triumphs, as well as others. There are styling similarities that would fit with many manufacturers. The photo is European and shows what appears to be a pennant flying on the front fender.

Sunbeam motorcycles were built at Wolverhampton, England from 1912-1957. The company from which they came is said to have had it's origins earlier than 1790 as a tinplate manufacturer. The company eventually produced bicycles and later motorcycles. The model shown here probably dates from the mid 1920s.

SUNBEAM

53

Motorcycling Through History

This is an advertising card for the Clyno motorcycle. The Clyno was built in England between 1909 and 1924, first in Northhamptonshire and later Woverhampton. The postcard is French, but the card was posted from New York to Ohio in May of 1919. The writer, W. Vallee-Picand is inquiring about exporting *"Brilliant Burners for motorcycles"* to France. His card is addressed to The Monosmith Co. in Spencer, Ohio.

With his pipe in place, his suit and tie on and his cap firmly placed on his head, this gentleman looks like he belongs behind a desk not sitting on the saddle of this great looking cycle. Unfortunately, I have not identified this machine. The rear passenger seat looks more comfortable than most that are seen on these early machines. There appears to be a large, rather strange looking battery box beneath the rider's seat which may power the lights and horn.

Here is a well outfitted rider on a cycle that has distinctly NSU characteristics. He appears to be a soldier and ready for the rigors of weather or war. His tall boots, riding suit and goggles should protect him from the weather at least. The postcard has never been posted or written on so unfortunately nothing else is know about the time or place of the picture.

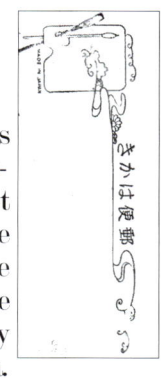

Chapter II: European Cycles

Vintage postcards from Asia with a motorcycle image are not too common. The cards on this page are all Japanese. The one at left is especially rare, featuring a ca. 1918 Harley-Davidson sitting next to *"The Aeroplane Niupol"*.

Shown here is a nice image of rural Japan. The characters at right say *"post card"*. The front caption describes the building as a *"Rental Library"*.

The card here appears to show 1929 Harley-Davidsons. Distinctive for that model year were the dual headlights that only lasted through the 1930 model year and the round tool box which was replaced in 1931 with a wedge shaped one. The characters on the front of the card read: *"Jan. 1st, Happy New Year."* This card was posted from Kyushu Island, Prefecture of Oita.

55

Motorcycling Through History

This daredevil couple are entertaining the crowds in Boston as they advertise their cycle and it's equipment.

"The Cycle Team Boston". Engine: J.A.P.
Gear change: Burman, Chain: Darbilly
Magneto: M.L, Carburetor: Amal, Oil: Celor

CARTE POSTALE

School days are a little more pleasant for this young man considering that he does not have to walk to get there. He appears pretty young to be out riding his own motorcycle. We can see that carrying a back pack is not a new thing for those going off to classes.

There is no doubt that this card has a subliminal message. It is an obvious advertisement for the durability of the suspension system on a DKW motorcycle. It is doubtful that this young German Fraulein is about to break any land speed records, although something mechanical looks as though it could give out. With a passenger things could really get crowded.

Chapter II: European Cycles

All of the cards on this page are European without any identifying information such as post marks or message. None has been posted or bears a stamp. Each has the plain, divided back with only the one at the bottom of the page having anything printed on it. The front of this card says: "On the way to Doorn." It was published by A. Grohs, Berlin, SW68

Triumph motorcycles were made in Germany by license from England and were very similar until the companies severed their relationship. Shown here is a ca. 1928 German, TWN, 248cc model. Triumphs were widely popular and produced in Germany from 1903-1957.

This very happy looking fellow reminds me of some of my sport bike riding friends. Give him a road with a lot of curves and he will be there testing the limits of his ability and that of the machine. His bug-catching smile is typical of most enthusiasts who dream of the open road and the pleasures that come along with that.

57

Motorcycling Through History

This wonderful image of an early Triumph cycle is especially nice for the tank decal shown below. This logo has been found on Triumph models as early as 1907. The rider of this cycle can be seen carrying a spare drive belt on the front spring. The photographer is shown to be Cyril Leighton, 101 Humberstone Rd. Leicester.

CARTE POSTALE

This divided back card was posted in France during 1912. The motorcycle is obviously not the main subject of the photo, but it is a nice side view of an early machine.

CARTE POSTALE

Published By: A. Michel, edit, 30 bis, pl. Bellecour, Lyon.

On this card is reference to the motorcycle repair shop of the professional school of the Catholic Mission at Togo-Lome. Motorcycle repair is obviously the focus for the African students. This card was never posted but probably dates from the same period as the one above.

Chapter II: European Cycles

This photograph is attributed to Jas. Freeman, Hounslow (England). The well dressed gentleman is sitting astride a mid 1920s BSA. It probably dates from about 1924-1927. This cycle has a single cylinder, overhead valve engine. Throughout the 1920s and 1930s, BSA made a variety of engines including side valve and overhead valve singles, and V-twins. Engine sizes in this period ranged from 174cc two strokes to 986cc V-twins.

The FN motorcycle was built in Belgium as early as 1901. It used a shaft drive and inline 4 cylinder engine. This is a pre-1924 model since it still has the shaft drive which was eliminated that year.

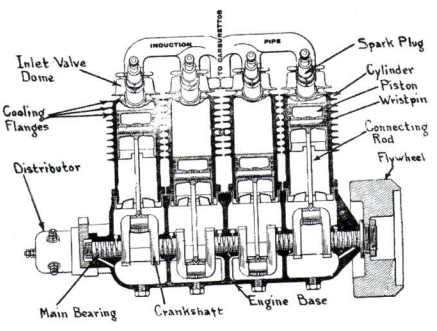

POSTKAART

HELPT ONS - WORDT LID.
Koninklijke Maatschappij tot bescherming der dieren
(Vereniging zonder winstgevend doel) POELDEMARKT, 7, GENT.

Over the years, the motorcycle was used in many ways to facilitate moving things other than people. This version shows how the motorcycle can be adapted to push a load. Sidecar arrangements were more common, but this method seems to work very well. This card came from the Netherlands.

59

Motorcycling Through History

This well dressed young man is sitting on a ca. 1920 Velocette. This machine was one of a number of models that Veloce Ltd. manufactured as the "everyman" motorcycle. This theme was carried out over the next five decades with production of the LE series (little engine) from 1949-1969. The leg shields as shown here were standard on these simple, commuter machines. Note the cute headlight ornament.

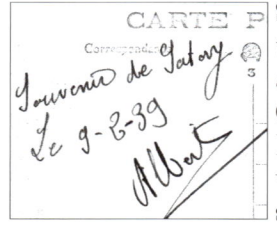

Shown in this photo are a pair of Gnome & Rhone cycles with factory sidecars. These are probably 1938 models. These machines were built in France between 1919 and 1959. The models shown had 750cc OHV, flat twin horizontally opposed engines. They were know as the "Model X".

This soldier is standing next to his ca. 1912 Rudge Multi. It was named Multi because of the large number of gear ratios offered. The Rudge company had roots back as far as 1868 when Dan Rudge began building Velocipedes, the forerunner of the bicycle. After his death the company went through a number of name changes before becoming Rudge-Whitworth Ltd. in 1894. The company was located at Crow Lane, Coventry where it survived until 1940.

Chapter II: European Cycles

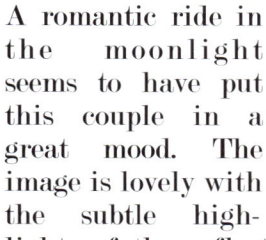

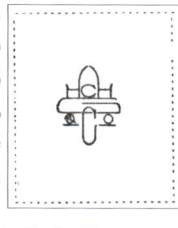

A romantic ride in the moonlight seems to have put this couple in a great mood. The image is lovely with the subtle highlights of the reflected full moon in the riders faces. This card was printed in Switzerland, probably in the late teens of the last century. The motorcycle is European, but the romance is universal.

Minerva motorcycles were made at Antwerp, Belgium from as early as 1901. The company built complete machines and provided their engines to many different manufacturers. This single cylinder example probably dates from between 1904 and 1906.

Note the rather radical V-twin configuration on this NSU cycle. It's 45 degree angle with the rear cylinder vertical is very unique and allowed better cooling for the rear cylinder.

61

Motorcycling Through History

The message on this card indicates it was posted to Amsterdam in 1920. Shown on the front is a ca. 1920 Triumph Jr., known as the "Baby". It was a 225 cc Type "LW" built by Triumph between 1914 and 1925, the smallest of the Triumph family of motorcycles.

The Rover motorcycle factory was founded in 1885 by James Starley as a bicycle manufacturer in Coventry. In 1901 plans were started for a motorcycle, and in 1903 a machine was introduced. Due to low sales, only 1250 machines were made and production stopped in 1905 replaced by clip-on engines in bicycle frames. Later on, motorcycles were again made but finally ended in 1925.

In 1908 this card was posted from France. The front end shot of the motorcycle makes identifying it extremely difficult. The cars are particularly interesting and should be easier to identify for automobile enthusiasts.

Société J. JOUGLA. - Paris.

62

Chapter II: European Cycles

Published by W.J. WELLSTED and SON, Photographer, BULL

POST CARD — CORRESPONDENCE — ADDRESS ONLY

Here is a turn-of-the-century photo that is amazingly sharp and detailed. From the image of the forecar at the upper left to all of the spectators, it is wonderful. The woman posing is standing beside her special ladies cycle. It is powered by a single cylinder JAP engine which was used in a great many makes of cycles.

This is a German made cycle car called a Cyclonette. It was built from 1905 until 1920. It's massive twin cylinder engine with it's large external flywheel is truly unique. A row of valves can be seen at the front of the engine being the intake and exhaust. The exhaust muffler is quite obvious as seen up front of the engine. The front wheel on this machine served both for steering and driving the cycle. It is said that this machine actually handled quite well.

Lichtdruck von Jos. Drotleff, Hermannstadt.

Post Card — For Correspondence — Address Only

Raleigh motorcycles were made at Nottingham, England as early as 1899. Primarily, the company made bicycles, and motorcycle production was sporadic. The peak years for cycles were the 1920s. The model shown here is from that era and probably early in the decade. It is an extremely clear photo of an historic British machine.

63

Motorcycling Through History

One of the most revered motorcycles in British history was the Rex which is represented in this photo attributed to E.J. Lee, The Studio, Irthlingborough. Rex cycles were made in England from 1903-1933. Singles and large V-twins were produced. In 1922 the company merged with Acme to become the Rex-Acme Co. A variety of engines were used over the years with displacements up to 998cc.

Early BMW postcards are extremely hard to find and this one is an exceptionally nice example. It is most likely a 1929 R16 ohv machine and has "Carlos Rozos" written in pencil on the back. On the front, the photo is attributed to "Gabspain" The card was obtained from Argentina.

Adler motorcycles were made in Germany between 1900 and 1957. This is an early machine, perhaps from as early as 1907. After that year and until 1939 the company shifted their production more to cars, typewriters and bicycles. After 1939 motorcycles again became a serious product. Early machines had 3-5hp Adler engines.

64

Chapter II: European Cycles

The young man smiling at us here is sitting on what is most likely a 1914-1919 Type H, Triumph Roadster. It had a 4 h.p. engine rated at 550cc. The suspension included the Triumph patented spring forks. The tank was enameled gray, the frame black and components heavily plated.

This wonderful period photograph shows what in all likelihood is an example of an early FN cycle. This is a pre-1924 model because that year the company switched to chain drives instead of the shaft drive shown here. The composition of this photo is great with emphasis on things mechanical. Along the back wall appear to be wicker storage baskets. Since the FN was made in Belgium this photo may originate from there.

Now, this is a machine you do not see every day. A rare image indeed. Whether this was a production model or a home made tricar, is hard to tell. It is believed to have been made for disabled riders. The source from whom the card was obtained identified the machine as a Jawa. The card came from the Czech Republic where the Jawa has been built since 1929. Jawa was started by the arms company Frantisek Janecek of Prague using the German Wanderer design. The Jawa name is the first two letters of Janecek and Wanderer.

65

Motorcycling Through History

The former Czechoslovakia, now the Czech Republic has been a long time producer of motorcycles. The CZ has been around since 1932. The initials stand for Ceska Zbrojovka which translates to Czech Arms Factory. The pressed steel frame on the example shown here puts it as pre-WWII, probably mid 1930s.

Another of the world's early motorcycles was the Minerva. It was built in Belgium between 1901 & 1914. This company build their own motorcycles as well as supplied engines to other manufacturers. A knowledgeable source has identified this engine as 1904 and the frame (not Minerva) to be Ca. 1905-1910. The name Minerva is visible on both the engine case as well as the gas tank. Minerva built engine kits that it sold in many European countries. The number plate indicates that this cycle was registered in Belgium.

John Alfred Prestwich was an engine builder from London, England. He gained great fame supplying his engines to a variety of motorcycle makers including Triumph, Matchless and Brough-Superior. Sold under the J.A.P. name, these engines went into a great many machines. It is uncertain as to who built the machine shown here.

66

Chapter II: European Cycles

The motorcycle shown in this photo is quite unusual. It was built in Belgium and was known as a "Spring". These machines were made between 1910 and 1940. After 1920 the cycles were equipped with transverse mounted V-twin engines as shown in this photo. Only one cylinder can be seen, angled away from the left side of the motorcycle. Models ranged in size up to nearly 1000cc and most were made for sidecar use.

This German Zundapp cycle was probably made in 1929 as a TS model K 249. The 249 referred to the displacement of 249cc. Production of the Zundapp began in 1917 and a great many models and design changes were seen throughout it's history. During the war years Zundapp saw a great deal of military use by the German Army. Those machines were heavy, sidecar hauling machines that had 746cc transverse mounted, flat twin engines.

In 1903 the Husqvarna company of Sweden was founded, originally as an arms factory. Motorcycles became and still are a major part of this company's history. Early machines were large V-twins, but in the 1930s a variety of singles came on the market like the one shown here. "Husky's" Are often favored for moto-cross racing.

Motorcycling Through History

Here is Aunt Clara aka "Miff" sitting astride her handsome motorcycle. She seems well enough dressed to face the cold wind and certain chill of a ride.

"Think of your little boy now. I have ridden many hundreds of miles on my motor. It is a champion. I have a sidecar as well. I had Amy with me all the way to Manchester about a month ago". So comments the man on this ca. 1915-1920 Rover motorcycle. The Rover was built at West Orchard, Coventry, England. This model had a 499cc engine of Rover's own design.

Looks like a motorcycle outing is about to take place as shown by this grouping of enthusiasts. This is a great period photo from about 1913. The two cycles on the right of the photo are Ariel's and date from that period. The wicker sidecar is nicely displayed. There are only two women visible in the photo and they are likely passengers. Cycling was still a boy's club.

68

Chapter II: European Cycles

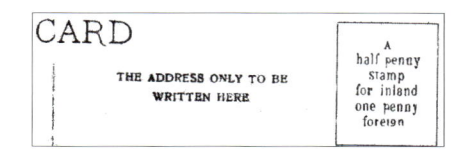

Most of the identifying features of this cycle are hidden, but those that appear seem to point to the A.J.S motorcycle. The A. J. Stevens & Co. Ltd. was founded in 1909 at Wolverhampton, England. If this is an A.J.S. it is most likely one of the very early models.

Aug 1914

The machine shown here appears to be an early Rover. They were made in England between 1902 and 1925. Characteristic of their design was the diamond shape frame, Druid fork with coil spring, and large muffler canister located between the rear down tube and the rear fender. These were well built machines that used side valve, single cylinder engines of 496cc as is shown here in a pre-1914 model. It's a very nice picture of an uncommon cycle.

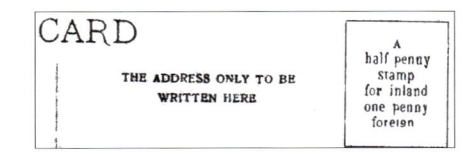

The Douglas company came into being in 1882 as a general engineering firm. In 1907 a motorcycle department was established. The horizontally opposed engine shown in the example here was unique. This machine could be from as early as 1910. The horizontal engine was named the Fee which was French for Fairy. Thus came the "Fairy" engine.

69

As seen on other pages of this book, Triumph motorcycle come in quite a variety of models. Most people would not recognize this as a Triumph if they are thinking British. The Triumph was made in Germany for many years following very similar lines to it's British counterpart. The model shown here is the K3 which may have been strictly a German design. It's large outside flywheel sets it apart from most other Triumphs. This machine is probably from the first half of the 1920s.

If you had lived in Belgium during the first half of the last century, you would have been familiar with the Sarolea motorcycle. It was built there between 1898 and 1957. The model shown is from the early 1920s when both 346cc and 496cc side valve and overhead valve singles were built. Sarolea was one of the earliest motorcycle manufacturers and lasted far longer than most.

At right is Alex Fraser and his ca. 1919 Rudge Multi. The card reads: *"Alec Fraser was born in Cupar, Fife, ran away from school and joined a touring Co. of "The Belle of New York" Since then he has played in comedy, drama and light opera at the Savoy, Lyceum, Lyric, Gaiety, Dalys and other west-end theatres. He has played in the following films" "The Will", "The Gamble in Lives", "The Knave of Diamonds", "The Woman of his Dreams", "The Woman With the Fan" "Little Brother of God", and "Beside the Bonnie Brier Bush." He is an enthusiastic Rudge rider."*

70

CHAPTER III:
RACING

Motorcycling Through History

Shown here is a wonderful artist rendition of early motorcycle racing and a very rare card. The card celebrates the anniversary of Continental, a manufacturer of tires. These strange looking motorcycles were most often used as pace bikes for bicycle races.

This card was posted on 28 Feb. 1911 and is quite a rare card.

Seen here is an extremely sharp and detailed view of a bicycle pace cycle. Seen here on the board track are two riders, the motorcyclist on his massive twin cylinder machine and the bicyclist close behind riding in the draft created by the pace cycle. The high banked board track is clearly seen in the background.

72

Chapter III: Racing

This strange looking motorcycle functioned as a "draft bike." or "pacing bike". In bicycle racing it was used to create a slip stream in front of the cyclist thus reducing the rider's effort and increasing his speed. Posted on 7 Oct. 1912 this card was sent from Neustadt Germany to Rhode Island.

INVER

Postbus 374
8300 AJ Emmeloord

The massive V twin engine in this pace cycle undoubtedly provides more than enough horse power and torque to stay ahead of the bicyclist. It seems a bit overkill, but these designs were commonplace in bicycle racing. The motorcycle is a Goricke from 1907.

In 1904 Germany, when this photo was taken, motorcycling was still in its infancy. Bicycle racing was extremely popular and these "pace bikes" often seemed huge and unwieldy. The written note under the cycle indicates 115 KPH.

73

Motorcycling Through History

Postkarte.

On 20 March 1906 this Card was posted in Germany. Cards showing the sport of bicycle racing using a pace cycle are fairly common, the majority of which are European.

Kurt Rosenlöcher, Dresden, hinter seinem Schrittmacher Starke.

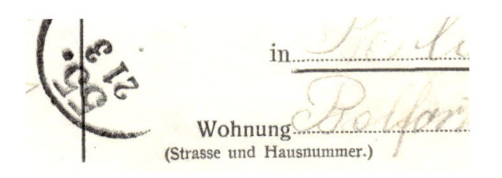

Bicycle racing was a huge sport at the start of the last century. This group of riders are portrayed on a card that says "*The most important flyer and duration driver*". Apparently the flyers or cyclists are shown here. This card was posted in 1911 and is very desirable.

Die bedeutendsten Flieger und Dauerfahrer der Welt, fahren Continental-Pneumatik

"*Gulgnard only rides Gurliches Westfal bikes*". Paul Gulgnard, holder of the world record time of 95.026 kilometers. Winner of the big gold bike trophy in Berlin-Steglitz 1907." The conversion for this record is 59.047 miles.

Berühmte Rennfahrer, Serie V. Guignard fährt nur Göricke's Westfalen-Rad

Paul Guignard, Inhaber des Stunden-Weltrecords mit 95,026 km, Gewinner des Grossen goldenen Rades von Berlin-Steglitz 1907

74

Chapter III: Racing

This card was posted to an address in France, unfortunately the date of the cancel cannot be read. It is most likely from the early teens of the last century. The rider is identified as Lanfranchi and noted is his record of 100 kilometres, 1/4 de litre. He may be riding the French made Werner which was built in Paris between 1897 & 1908 by two Russian brothers, Michel & Eugene Werner.

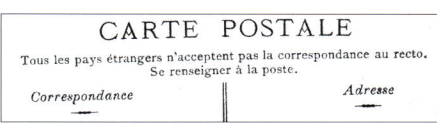

Olieslaegers, " Le Demon Belge" champion du monde, sur Motocyclette "L'albatros" Pneus "Le Persan". This champion board track racer is proudly wearing a shirt that says "ALBATROS". Early racing cards like this and those found on the next few pages are very collectible and bring good prices.

If one looks very closely at this picture, wires can be seen supporting both the motorcycle and the bicycle so that a nice, clear photo could be obtained. The bicyclist was pulled along in the slip stream so that maximum speed could be obtained. The gas tank on this machine is set at an unusual angle to facilitate the flow of gasoline to the engine. Or do you suppose that the tank is set to make a visual statement about the riders masculinity?

75

Motorcycling Through History

This French card and the one below show riders in nice, close up photographs which is quite unusual to find. Because films of the day were not nearly as fast as today, action shots were difficult to capture. It is believed that some of these type of pictures were staged and thin wires held the motorcycle and rider stationary for the picture. This rider is identified as Danglard. The card was not been posted and no date information is available. The machine dates from the early 20th century pre-teen years.

This photo, probably taken at the same time as the one above is especially sharp and detailed. The rider is identified as Pernette. Board track racers always had to be fearful of nails and the ends of boards sticking up. Protective riding gear was primitive and serious accidents often occurred.

Handwriting on the back of this card identifies the individual as Ed Whittles. This is a great close-up photo at the board track with him sitting on a Peugeot V-twin. Made in France since 1899 these cycles were great racing machines. In 1913 Peugeot introduced 494cc vertical twins with double overhead cam engines. The machine shown dates from that era.

76

Chapter III: Racing

Shown here is another picture of the rider Pernette seen on the previous page. What a great front on view nicely posed with the support wires visible that are holding the rider and machine in place.

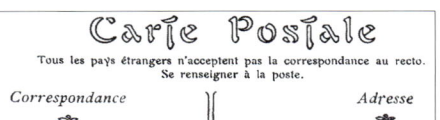

Apparently there are quite a number of cards in this series. They are not very common and always bring strong prices on auction sites. The publisher has done a great job of capturing the excitement of early board track racing and preserving the history of some of the more famous riders of the time.

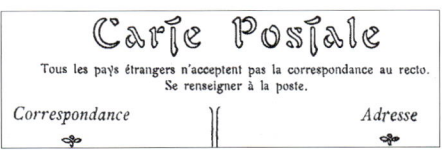

A reference to this rider was found on the Internet that indicated that he was a world champion rider in 1900. An article appears to have been written about him in a French publication, but that information could not be found.

Motorcycling Through History

This rider is identified as Giuppone representing Italy. Records have been found that mention a Giuppone riding a Peugeot in the 1909 T.T., riding 500 single cylinder and 750 twin machines. He is looking pretty dapper in his cap and tweed jacket. The boots seem to be his only concession to riding safety.

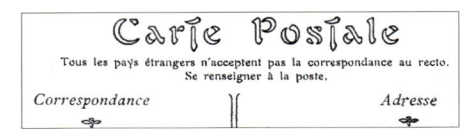

Rene Champoiseau was active in early 20th century racing. At the XIII Grand Prix de l'A.C.F. on 12 July 1913 at Amiens, he rode to a seventh place finish on a Th Schneider, with a time of 8 hours, 44 min. and 32.6 seconds. The distance was 916.98 km which amounted to 29 laps of 31.62 km each. He finished 51 minutes behind the first place winner.

Norton motorcycles began their life with the first model in 1902. They were the product of James Lansdowne Norton an apprenticed toolmaker. He joined with Charles Riley Garrard to create that first, of a very long line of Nortons. The one shown here is probably a 1928-1929 model. A long history of racing achievements marked Norton's rise in popularity. This stripped down Norton is obviously set up for the race track.

Chapter III: Racing

One of the early and great events in motorcycling was board track racing. Steeply inclined wooden tracks were built to challenge riders to push the limits of their machines. At left is a nice photo depicting a race at Luna Park. This card was published by the Century Post Card Co., Cleveland, Ohio and was posted in 1913.

This is another view of Luna Park showing a nice overview of the track. Part of the message on the reverse reads: *"Was out to Luna Park last night.. Went to see races at motor dome, but were called off on acct. of a little rain. Cost 2 bits just the same. Two fellows got hurt in the practice".* This card and the similar one's shown are eagerly collected.

The two views above this show typical board track action. In this picture the track has flattened out and become dirt. It is December 21, 1916 at *"Motorcycle Races and Aeroplane, Driving Park, Lima, O."* Perhaps when the bikes were not racing the airplanes could land & Taxi.

Pub. by the Webb Book & Bible Co.

Motorcycling Through History

"Crash on the dirt track"

The image shown here is as real now as it was in 1931 when it was created. The artist has done a great job of bringing out the drama of dirt track racing. These artist rendered cards are particularly attractive and collectible.

— Verlag: Percy Hein, München 2 —
Tom Fischer: Sturz auf der Aschenbahn

This card was made in England and says *"Supplement to "Triumph," 17/10/36"* The text on the back is as follows: *"J.S. Wright set up a world's motorcycling record (since broken) when, on Nov. 7th 1930, he reached a speed of 150.736 miles an hour, at Cork, Ireland. He rode an O.E.C. Temple-Jap, the design of Mr. Temple, the first man to travel at 100 m.p.h. on a mo'-bike."* O.E.C. built motorcycles from 1901-1954 using various engines. Joe Wright rode a supercharged O.E.C. with an 85 bhp, 996cc V-twin ohv JAP engine.

In the history of motorcycle racing, "the wall of death" is one of the daredevil events that never fails to generate excitement. This card portrays the event with it's macabre warning in each corner. The card is from Bulgaria and reads " First Bulgarian champion, Mr. Gligor Ivanov Sokolov who motorcycled on vertical wall". This may not be a true postcard since there is nothing at all printed on the back, but it is a very unique image dramatizing the danger of the sport.

Chapter III: Racing

Org. 3 Eros
Schreckenfahrt m. Motorrädern an steiler Wand

Motorcyclists never fail to find some unique way to endanger their lives. The "Wheel of Death" was one of those creations. Unlike later, more substantial versions, this early Germany wheel looks particularly shaky. The riders normally start at the bottom building speed and momentum until they have climbed the vertical walls. The two cyclists here seem to have reached the safety of a platform.

Lübecker Lichtdr.-Anst. Schmidt & Gebr. Böttger, Lübeck, Postfach 224

G.M. GREEN CROSSING THE FINISHING LINE TRAVELING AT THE RATE OF 71 MILES PER HOUR, WALTHAM ROAD RACE SEPT 7TH 1908, ON HIS M-M 7 H.P. TWIN BUILT BY AMERICAN MOTOR CO. BROCKTON MASS.

Post Card

"*G.M. Green crossing the finishing line traveling at the rate of 71 miles per hour, Waltham road race, Sept. 7th 1908 on his M.M. 7 H.P. twin built by American Motor Co. Brockton Mass.*"

Reverse of card is advertisement for the M.M. cycle.

Ride an
M·M BATTERY "4"
Built by AMERICAN MOTOR CO.
Brockton, Mass.

GRAND PRIX DE FRANCE DES MOTOCYCLETTES. — CIRCUIT DE FONTAINEBLEAU, 22 JUIN 1913.
MILLAND SUR MOTOSACOCHE ET PNEUS HUTCHINSON, GAGNANT DE LA CATÉGORIE DES 750 CM3 SIDE-CARS, BATTANT LES SIDE-CARS DE 1.000 CM3.
Edition du Pneu Hutchinson

Sidecar racing has a long history and this image portrays it at one of it's earliest stages. The race shown here was run on 22 June 1913. The rider named Hutchinson was racing in the 750cc and 1000cc sidecar categories at Fontainebleau riding a French made Motosacoche. Today, sidecar racers carry a passenger known as the "monkey" who has the job of leaning out as far as possible to maintain stability on corners where precarious things can happen if speed and centrifugal force combine in the right amounts.

Motorcycling Through History

The Sears motorcycle was built for the Sears Roebuck company between 1910 and 1916. The early machines used Thor engines as shown in this photo. Later machines incorporated engines by the Excelsior Cycle Co. of Chicago which built the "Deluxe" motorcycle. This card No. 13430 shows *"The record breaking Sears Motorcycle, Sears, Roebuck & Co's exhibit, Illinois State Fair Grounds, Springfield, Ill."*

"The Yale Team, winners of the Chicago motorcycle club endurance contest, July 9, 10 and 11. 600 miles at an average speed of 20 miles per hour, without making a single adjustment. awarded the silver trophy cup. This is the world's record endurance. Investigate before buying. The consolidated Mfg. Co., Toledo, Ohio." The riders, L-R are W. Ingram, S.J. Chubbuck and A.R. Oberwegner. The card was posted on Jan. 4th, 1910 at Toledo and was made by the Chilton Publishing Co.., Phila., Pa. U.S.A

This is a great advertising card for the Emblem Mfg. Co. It reads: *"Emblem Motorcycle winning first race ever run in the United States between a motorcycle and a flying machine. L.S. Taylor, rider, at Columbus, Ohio, October 8, 1910– 2 miles. Time: 2 min. 5 seconds."* The card was made by the Chilton Company, Philla., PA. U.S.A. 3940. It was used to acknowledge order receipts and promised *"earliest possible ship date."* Emblem Mfg. Co. Angola, (Erie Co.) N.Y."

82

CHAPTER IV: SIDECARS

Motorcycling Through History

Harley-Davidson has always provided a means for family transportation. From the earliest years until the year 2004 they are still a standard factory product. The family picture shown here is a great portrait from the first quarter of the last century. The lady shown with her baby seems to be taking life in stride under the watchful eye of all of her men. No family information is provided on this card. Where are the rest of the women in this family?

When family transportation was considered, one wonders if Harley-Davidson pictured the family at right as a typical customer. Here is Mr. Ben Walker and the City Bloodhounds, Fort Smith Ark. Phone 3223. The reverse adds: *"I have returned from the Army and am ready and at your service any time you should need me. Sincerely Yours, Ben Walker and the City Bloodhounds."*

Riding an Indian sidecar rig, this well-to-do looking couple look ready for a Sunday ride in the country. The photo was taken by F.J. Foill, Jackson, Michigan and his name is embossed into the front of the card. There is no message and the card has not been posted. The motorcycle probably dates from around 1915.

84

Chapter IV: Sidecars

At left and below are wonderful scenes that would stir the restless nature of any avid motorcyclist seeking a new road and great scenery. The center dividing line says "Agfa". Imprinted on the front is "Santiago de Cuba No. 92 Carretera Central National Highway". It is only a guess, but this rider is probably riding an early Harley-Davidson. This guess is based on the characteristic shape of the sidecar visible under a magnifying glass.

Traveling roads through breathtaking scenery is one of the joys of motorcycling. The view here is in Wales and the caption reads *"Bwlch-Y-Groes, Nr Bala, Gradient 1 in 4"*.

85

Motorcycling Through History

This sidecar rig definitely seems to be a German Zundapp. The leg shields are a bit of a hindrance to identification. It appears that the engine is a vertical twin, not the typical Zundapp engine.

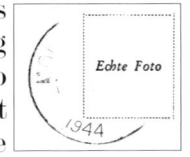

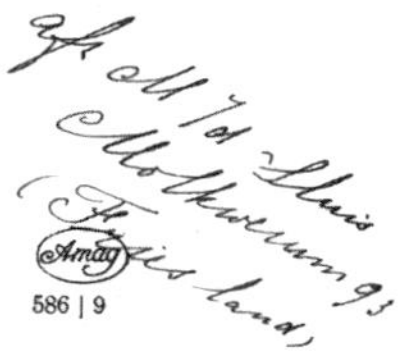

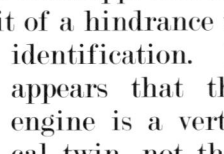

Here is a young soldier who obviously has his mind on his sweetheart at home. He is sitting on his Eysink motorcycle which was made in the Netherlands towards the end of the 1930s. This machine probably has a Villiers engine installed.

The couple shown here are about to get on their mid to late 1930s Zundapp cycle. This appears to be a 746 cc, flat twin engine with transverse mounting. This was the typical design for the larger displacement Zundapp's of that era. A flat four cylinder was also produced. These machines saw heavy military use.

86

Chapter IV: Sidecars

On this page are a series of cards from the Netherlands. The card at left and the one below it are posed with the same couple and sentiment, *"Leaving on Vacation."* The motorcycle is a DKW from the 1930s. Made in Germany since 1919, the DKW was, during the 1930s the largest manufacturer of motorcycles in the world.

No. 497/3   *Amag*

Here is another view of the same couple as shown above. The date is a little later indicated by the postmark, but in all likelihood the photo's were taken at the same time. This card was posted from Amsterdam on June 23, 1938 and is Amag card No. 599/5.

This looks like another happy couple out for a ride. The card is an Amag card No. 663/5. It has been posted, but the stamp has been removed taking with it the date. The caption reads:

"A motorcycle with sidecar is only for two, but here, happiness is number 3."

87

Motorcycling Through History

The Rene-Gillet was a French motorcycle that was built between 1898 and 1957. They were very popular for sidecar use because they were heavy and powerful machines. The sidecar in this photo is quite attractive with the neat pin stripe decoration, but it is not a Rene-Gillet factory item. This is a 750cc Twin cylinder model that was available in the 1930s.

The motorcycle in this photo is not identified, but the sidecar is a Steib which is a very popular German brand. Classic Steib sidecars are prized and quite valuable. This card was posted in 1939 from Tholen in the Netherlands. It is card No. 604/14.

These three British soldiers seem especially happy. The names, Johnson, Milton, and Grooms, are penned on the back of the photo. In addition a pencil notation says "Northamptonshire Reg." This card has not been posted but probably dates from the late teens.

Chapter IV: Sidecars

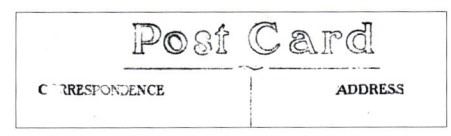

Sidecars have been a part of motorcycling since the beginnings of the sport. Many cycle manufacturers made sidecars to mount directly on their machines while many other companies specialized in just making sidecars. This photograph of an English family shows them on what appears to be an early New Hudson cycle.

Shown here is a happy family at the Clifton Baths and Bathing Pool, Cliftonville, England. The photo was taken by J. Easton in 1930. Although the cycle appears to say JAP on the gas tank, this manufacturer of motorcycle engines made very few complete cycles and only in the earliest years. Their engines were used in a great many different motorcycles including the famous Brough Superior. This rig was probably a prop for photo taking since other cards with different people have been seen.

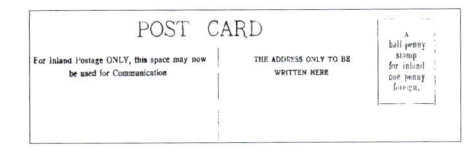

At left is a very handsome sidecar mounted to an unidentified cycle. This nice photo was taken in England. The card was never posted and has space for a 1/2 penny stamp. The wicker work and upholstery on this rig are extremely nice and a well dressed lady companion would be kept nicely protected from most road dirt.

Motorcycling Through History

The German riding team shown here are on a Mars cycle which was built in Germany between 1903 and 1957. This model probably dates from about 1920-1923. The photo was taken at Magdeburg, Germany which is on the Elbe River and approx. 82 miles WSW of Berlin. In the background and depicted in the hand stamp on the front is most likely the 13th century cathedral found there. The card is by H. Hansen, Magdeburg, Kl. Junkestr. 7.II. It also reads: "Von Magdeburg nach Magdeburg 12000 km

The card at right is most likely German although nothing identifying is found on the back. The happy expression on the face of the young lady is in stark contrast to the stern appearances of the adults. Is mother the boss of this family or has dad put himself in the position of authority by directing his lady to haul him around? For the young lady it does not seem to matter as she seems happy with her place in the family. The shape of this sidecar is quite interesting.

This card shows an interesting scene from January of 1928. It was posted from Jerusalem to an address in Leipzig, Germany. The sender is probably the man in the photo who appears to be on a motorcycle adventure. The sidecar clearly shows the destinations as Berlin and Kairo (Cairo, Egypt).

90

Chapter IV: Sidecars

Few early real photo post cards are as sharp and clear as this one. These early teens Triumphs with their wicker sidecars were very fashionable at the time. The handsome men and their beautiful ladies provide a striking image of a time when motorcycles were thought of much differently than today. A hand written message on the back says: *"Friendship brings friends nearer, making friendship dearer, Love, Ben & Lou to Edi"*

The Triumph shown here is quite a bit newer than those above. This one probably dates from 1930-1931. It is very likely that this model is a 647cc vertical twin which was designed for the sidecar market. This sidecar was a factory made item. The rig was highly acclaimed but did not have a strong following and sales dwindled. This postcard has a divided back and *Agfa* is printed into the center dividing line.

At left is a very interesting motorcycle with it's comfortable sidecar. Identifying the cycle has been a challenge and although it has a great many similarities to a German made Komet of about 1905, that is not certain. The front forks, the gas tank design and the extremely long handlebar levers all say Komet. The card is European with the words "postcard" written in 23 different languages.

91

Motorcycling Through History

This wonderful photo shows a very proper English couple out for a ride in the country. The motorcycle is probably an early Ariel. The first two-wheeled Arial cycles came out around 1902. The machine shown in this photo probably dates from the pre-teens of the last century.

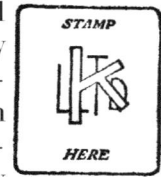

Biker babes from yesteryear

The only available information on this card is the name, Mr. Jonas Fox, penciled into the address side of the back. The two ladies are sitting on an early Harley-Davidson rig. It probably dates from around 1916-1918. The sidecar is distinctly Harley and from the same era as the motorcycle.

This is quite an impressive looking rig. It's three happy riders look as though they could all snuggle comfortably into the sidecar together. This is probably a European postcard and it would seem that the motorcycle would be easy to identify. So far that has not been the case. The sidecar is distinctive with it's nose so high in the air. Seeing over the windshield cannot be very easy.

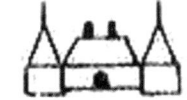

92

Chapter IV: Sidecars

> POST CARD
> CORRESPONDENCE   ADDRESS

Could this be dad and his son posing for the camera? The young lad appears to be happy in the drivers seat. He is sitting on a ca. 1914 Douglas cycle. The location is certainly England, but no information is provided.

The BMW shown above is probably a 1938 R71. At 745cc it was the largest of the 1938 models and designed for sidecar use. This photo appears to be of Hungarian origin.

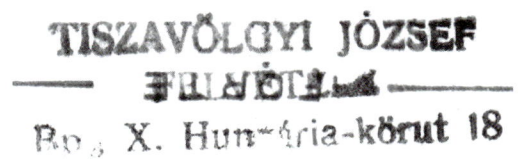

> TISZAVÖLGYI JÓZSEF
> — FIGRTE —
> Bp. X. Hungária-körut 18

These handsome looking canines seem right at home on their masters Indian, sidecar rig. Dating from around 1913 to 1914 this rig stands out nicely against the snow. It is not uncommon to see riders and their best canine friends out on the highway teamed up on a sidecar rig. Dogs seem to take to the thrill of riding as much as their owners.

> PLACE A STAMP HERE

93

Motorcycling Through History

Dressed in his finest clothes and derby hat, this gentleman sits relaxed upon his ca. 1914 Excelsior motorcycle. The wicker sidecar is a fine example of the quality work that was done at that time. The swing-out door made entry easy for the ladies and the plush upholstery was comfortable and inviting. The name "George" is written on the card.

By any standard, this English sidecar appears quite luxurious. The young lady is tucked in and appears very comfortable beside her beau. He too seems quite ready for a ride. This photo probably dates from the mid to late teens of the last century. For all of us who think that wearing one's cap backwards is a new phenomenon, just look at this young fellow. Of course on a motorcycle the caps brim would make a perfect wind catcher necessitating the stop and chase procedure.

Although the Indian cycle is obscured in this picture, the Indian sidecar is nicely displayed. A faint Indian head logo can be seen on the door. This rig is probably from ca. 1913-1915. This riding team has a number of very interested observers as seen in the background.

Chapter IV: Sidecars

Shown below is an extremely nice family portrait. Perhaps grandpa is posing with his son and daughter-in-law and their baby. They are shown with a nice Harley rig. Unusual is the fact that the photo is Eastern European. The card was acquired from Estonia, but was not posted. The card is from the late teens of the 1900s.

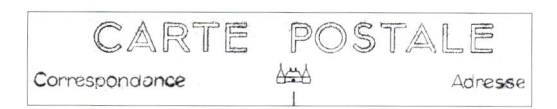

LEONAR 4135

CARTE POSTALE
Correspondance   Adresse

This posed photo is typical of many similar images taken in Eastern Europe. It is common to find a scene like this in front of an attractive back drop.

CARTE POSTALE

The front of this card is signed by the riders. In the sidecar is Z. Sulkowsky and on the bike is GY. Bartha. They have ridden over 5 continents and visited 64 countries between 1928 & 1935 covering a distance of 160,000 km. This grand voyage on motorcycle began in Budapest, Hungary.

Z. SULKOWSKY et GY. BARTHA
Le premier voyage complet autour du monde en moto.
160.000 km. de Budapest, Hongrie, 1928-1935, à travers
5 Continents et 64 pays.

95

Motorcycling Through History

In 1905, The Marsh brothers along with Charles Metz collaborated to form the American Motor Company. Marsh & Metz cycles also known as M.M. became popular and the company survived until 1913. The owners developed the first 90 degree V-twin engine in America, as shown in the example here. The V-twin first came out in 1908. This is a wonderful period photo with lovely wicker sidecar.

CARTE POSTALE

These French or Belgian riders are lined up nicely with their sidecar rigs. In the early days, wicker was the material of choice for these passenger transports. The middle car in this photo has what appears to be a convertible top rising part way, while the front of the car is covered with a tonneau cover.

"*Africa Christian series II, the trips of the missionary*".

Il « pichi-pichi », con velocità
Passa, e talvolta il re della foresta
Resta interdetto nelle male gesta
Da quell'arnese tutto novità.

"*Noise comes with the speed and sometimes the king of the jungle looks upset when the new machine is sounding bad*".

« L'Istituto Missioni Africane accoglie Giovanetti, Studenti e Fratelli Catechisti, desiderosi di consacrarsi all'Opera delle Missioni in Africa ».

"*The mission association Africa, receives young students and brother catechists who wish to work at the missions in Africa*".

GRAFICHE A.L.M.A. MILANO

96

CHAPTER V: ADVERTISING

Motorcycling Through History

Rudge-Whitworth cycles were extremely popular prior to 1940 when production ceased. They were highly regarded in racing circles and as seen here, adapted well to family situations. Note the rumble seat in the sidecar.

The Styria was made in Austria between 1905 and 1908 using Fafnir engines. This card was posted to Innsbruck in 1908 and is quite rare.

Ges.Qesch.Nachdruck Verboter Akt. Ges. F. Kunsidruck Niedersedliz.b. Dresden

If it were not for the postal cancel on this card, it would most likely not be considered a postcard. The weight of the paper is a bit thin and the back is plain without anything to indicate that it was made as a postcard. Even so, it is a nice piece of advertising for the Indian Motocycle. Most likely this advertisement appeared to introduce the 1909 models. This is a rare advertising image.

98

Chapter V: Advertising

Rudge motorcycles were built at Coventry, England from 1911-1940. They were a favored machine for racing in many countries and many TT, Grand Prix and other races were won on them. This halfpenny card with divided back is from a painting by Guy Lipscombe. It depicts racing at Brooklands, 1914 Senior TT.

La Francaise-Diamant was a French motorcycle that had it's origins in bicycle manufacturing. The company began buying engines that they attached to the frames of their bicycles before branching out to true motorcycles. The advertising card shown here marked the last models supplied by this manufacturer before being absorbed by the Alcyon Company which built a variety of motorcycles under various names like, Labor; Thomann; Alcyon; and Olympique, until 1957

Two separate reference books show the motorcycle at left to be spelled, Durandal. This advertising card shows the name and address of the agent in Barcelona, Spain. The Durandal motorcycle was built in France from around 1925-1932. Some models, like this one had a pressed steel frame. Engines were primarily JAP of 246cc— 490cc. A racing machine was also built using a KTT Velocette, ohc engine.

99

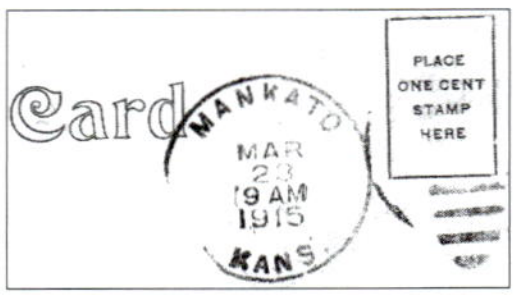

Motorcycling Through History

The advertising card shown here is a fairly common one put out by the Motorcycle Equipment Co. of Hammondsport, N.Y. MECO carried a vast array of motorcycle parts and accessories. The company was organized in 1904 and incorporated in 1910. This card was issued by the Pacific Coast Branch which was located at 3664 S. Main St. Los Angeles, CA.

CARTE POSTALE
The card shown here is advertising the Viratelle motorcycle. This machine was made in France between 1907 and 1924 at Lyon. The company address is shown on the reverse of the card.

SOCIETE ANONYME
Des Motocyclettes et Automobiles
"VIRATELLE"
7-9-11, Rue Jean-Bourgey, 7-9-11
LYON-VILLEURBANNE
(Rhone)

Identifying this machine has been an interesting quest. Going strictly by the name on the fuel tank has not helped. Under close magnification the name appears to read: Vulcain. This is a French word that has no reference in the motorcycle world. It is most notably associated with the French Ariane 5 rocket of the same name.

Chapter V: Advertising

This is an advertisement for the M & M motorcycle. The M. M. motorcycle was produced from 1906-1913 as a collaboration between Charles Metz and William Marsh. Metz had been a designer for the Orient bicycle company adding engines as early as 1898.

Ride an
M·M BATTERY "4"
Built by AMERICAN MOTOR CO.
Brockton, Mass.

At left is the M.M. Special for 1908. This card was posted from New York, N.Y. in March of 1908. And sent to Mr. Robert York in Maine. It reads *"Dear Rob, Buy a Marsh and know pleasure, don't buy a Marsh and no pleasure. Yours Truly, "Bunt"*. The cards on this page are occasionally seen and always valuable.

This advertising card for the M. M. motorcycle states: *"On the other side of this card we illustrate our famous M.M "4" which is, without doubt, the highest development in motorcycle construction. The following points (most of which are not possessed by any other machine) bear out this statement: automatic oiling system, roller bearings in motor, steel fly wheels, emergency tank, the original M.M. spring fork, comfortable to ride, positive control, simple in construction."*

Motorcycling Through History

The date on this card is written as May 2nd. 1916. It was written to *"Dear Little hazel, From Auntie Douglas"*. The connection to the Douglas name is probably coincidental. The reverse reads *"Douglas, dispatch riders no. 10"*.

Postcards have always been used as a medium for advertising and motorcycles were often found on cards of this type. Shown below is a nice card portraying a British made Douglas of ca. 1927. It had a 349cc side valve, flat twin engine.

Corp. E. HOOPER, R.E.
Despatch Rider
General Headquarters, B.E.F.

"The 'Douglas' in the photograph I rode through those awful winter months, and not once was I held up on the road for engine trouble. It is the handiest machine in France."

THE CLOISTERS
GLOUCESTER CATHEDRAL

Douglas
LEADER OF THE PACK

DOUGLAS MOTORS LTD., KINGSWOOD, BRISTOL

POSTKARTE
„HUY"
Fahrzeug- und Motorenbau
Inhaber: Walter Huy
DRESDEN-N. 22
Moritzburger Str. 19
Fernruf 27318

Modell L I
2 PS Viertakt, steuer- u. führerscheinfrei mit Zweiganggetriebe, Ketten- und Riemenantrieb
Modell L II
3 PS Viertakt, steuer- u. führerscheinfrei mit Zweiganggetriebe, Ketten- und Riemenantrieb
Modell S I
6 u. 8 PS Viertakt mit Dreiganggetriebe und Kettenantrieb
Spezial - Reparatur - Werkstätte

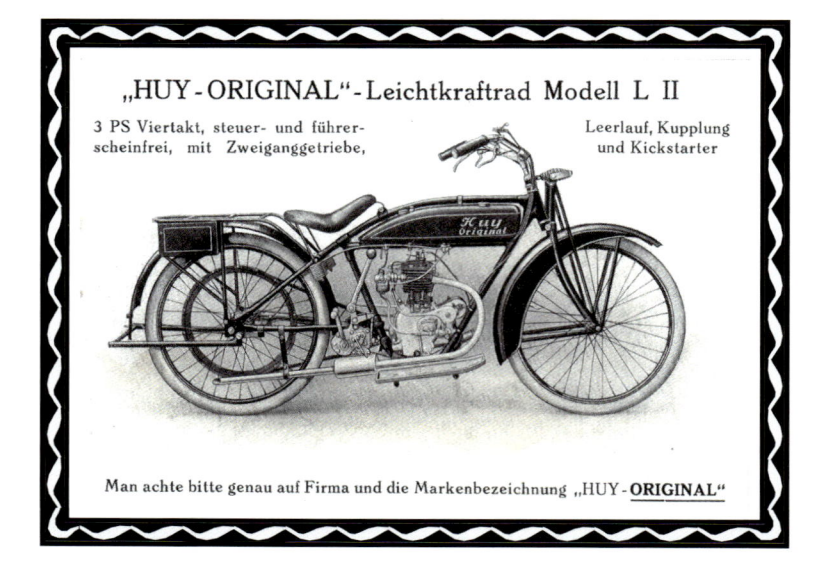

„HUY-ORIGINAL"-Leichtkraftrad Modell L II
3 PS Viertakt, steuer- und führerscheinfrei, mit Zweiganggetriebe, Leerlauf, Kupplung und Kickstarter

Man achte bitte genau auf Firma und die Markenbezeichnung „HUY-ORIGINAL"

Chapter V: Advertising

Left: Card posted April 1, 1910 from Brockton Mass. Reverse reads: *"I left Amsterdam Holland Feb. 1 1909 without money or luggage to go around the world. I have already finished Europe and will now cross the U.S.A. to San Francisco. From there to Yokohama, Japan, then through Japan and China, Siberia and Russia back to Holland in three and one half years. I was loaned this machine by the American Motor Co. of Brockton Mass. To ride across the country as an advertisement for the M.M. Motorcycle. Upon reaching San Francisco the machine will belong to me."*

Above is an early advertising card for Michelin Ballons (tires). It is a hand drawn image with the name "Frole", presumed to be the artist, seen under the saddle. Other letters are visible on each foot peg, but they cannot be read clearly. This may have been a privately printed card with nothing to indicate otherwise.

Left: *"Walter Goerke, Amateur Motorcyclist using an Eclipse free engine pulley at Cortlandt St. and Broadway, New York."* This card is from a series of advertising cards by the Eclipse Machine Co. This one was posted May 18, 1911 from Elmira N.Y. Printed by the Blanchard Press N.Y. it is card No. 30184

Motorcycling Through History

Right: Advertising card for the Eclipse Machine Co. Posted Jan. 27, 1911 at Elmira N.Y. Card reads: *"Jake DeRosier, professional champion of the United States, with an Eclipse coaster brake and free engine pulley on his motor cycle at Hotel Plaza, New York."* Photo by Irving Underhill, N.Y. Card 30177, Blanchard Press.

Above: *"A.C. Rice of the Eclipse Machine Co. nearing Trinity Church, New York, on a motorcycle equipped with an Eclipse free engine pulley."* Photo by A. Loeffler, Tompkinsville, New York. Card No. 30189, printed by the Blanchard Press, N.Y. Posted April 10, 1911 at Elmira, New York.

Right: *"Glenn H. Curtiss on his motorcycle equipped with the Eclipse free engine pulley, at Madison Avenue and Twenty Third Street, New York."* Printed by the Blanchard Press and posted from Elmira N.Y. on May 20, 1911. Card No. 30185.

Chapter V: Advertising

"*Miss Clara Wagner with her motorcycle at Coenties Slip, New York, using the Eclipse coaster brake.*" Photo by A. Loeffler, Tompkinsville N.Y. Card No. 30208. By the Blanchard Press. This series of cards all have a hand written or printed message from the Eclipse Machine Co. This card reads: "*Miss Clara Wagner the most successful and experienced motorcyclist always uses the Eclipse coaster brake. Miss Wagner states that the perfect security I felt on my brake equipment contributed largely to the pleasure.*"

"*Raymond Seymour, of Los Angeles, Cal., amateur world's champion on the speedway approaching Washington Bridge, New York, using an Eclipse free engine pulley and coaster brake on his motorcycle.*" This card was posted Dec. 30, 1910 from Elmira N.Y. and is No. 30174 in the series. This series of cards was done for both motorcycles and bicycles. They are always in demand and I am only aware of one motorcycle version that I do not have which is very rare.

BRIEFKART
(CARTE POSTALE)
ALGEMEENE POSTVEREENIGING
(UNION POSTALE UNIVERSELLE)
This card was posted Jan. 11, 1904 from The Netherlands. Translation reads: "*Fongers-Bicycles, The received impression has strengthened us in the conviction that the bicycle factory at Groninger produces good quality, a product that not just on the Dutch bicycle market, but also on the European one, stands up well. A Fongers bicycle is a good machine for a fair price. From: Dutch Sport Magazine of 19 Feb. 1898.*"

105

Motorcycling Through History

The front of this card shows an AJS sidecar rig from 1928. Posted in Czechoslovakia, the divided front of the card shows the photo and the postal cancel. The reverse has a typed message and the identifying stamp shown here.

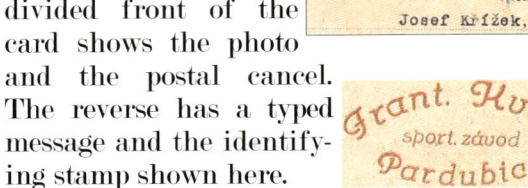

Below is a divided back card bearing No. 1203-30. This card advertises the ruggedness of the B.S.A. The rear advertising says: "*A B.S.A. 3.49 h.p., O.H.V. Motor Bicycle climbed Snowdon in 24 min. 6 sec.*" "*Lead the way on a B.S.A.*"

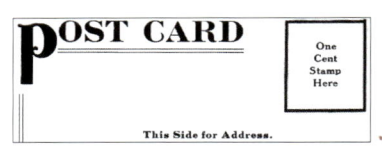

Yale motorcycles were the product of the Consolidated Mfg. Co. of Toledo, Ohio a bicycle manufacturer until 1903 when they bought out the California Motorcycle Co. Up until 1908 the cycles carried the Yale California name, but after that they became just Yale. Production stopped in 1915. The year 1911 is printed under the Yale name.

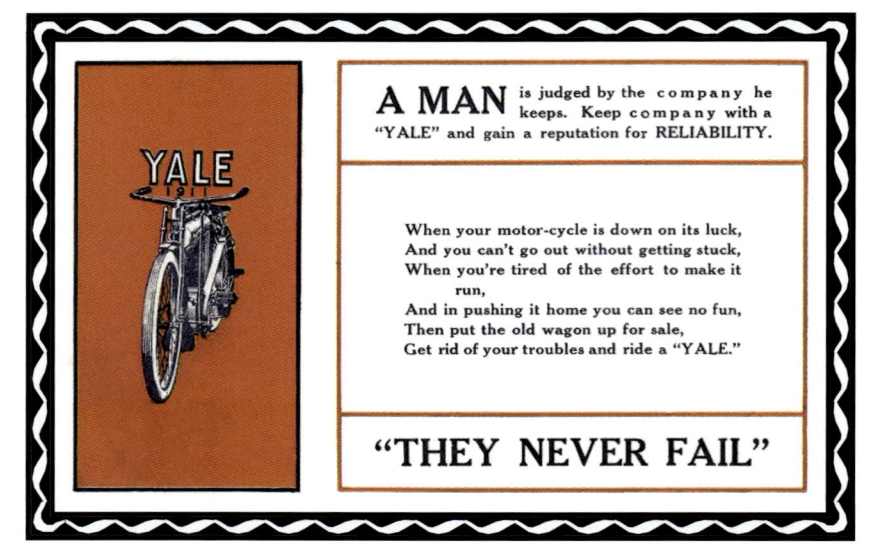

A MAN is judged by the company he keeps. Keep company with a "YALE" and gain a reputation for RELIABILITY.

When your motor-cycle is down on its luck,
And you can't go out without getting stuck,
When you're tired of the effort to make it run,
And in pushing it home you can see no fun,
Then put the old wagon up for sale,
Get rid of your troubles and ride a "YALE."

"THEY NEVER FAIL"

Chapter V: Advertising

In 1920, Indian introduced the "Scout" to it's line-up. This was a mid-size twin of 600cc that was targeted at customers intimidated by the larger V-twins and as a good introductory model for those just getting into motorcycling. Designed by Charles Franklin, the "Scout" may have been the pinnacle of his engineering success. The machine was extremely reliable with innovative features.

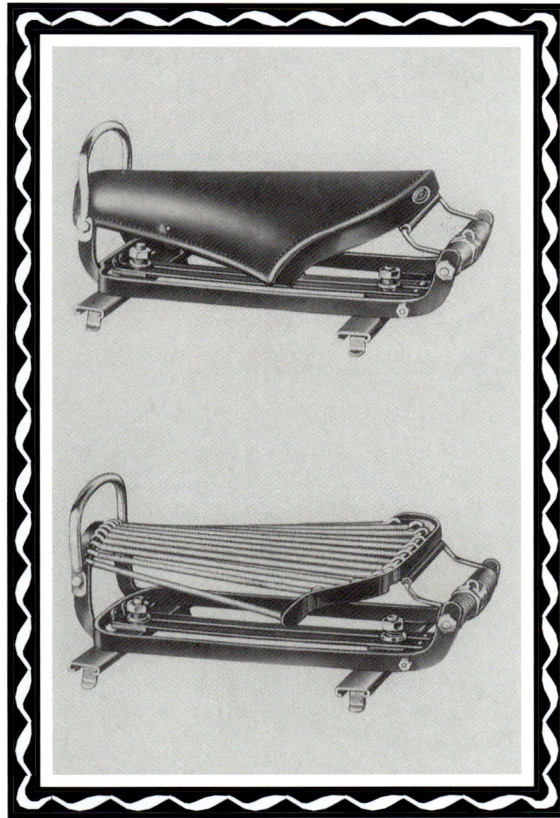

At left is the back of the Indian card shown above it.

"Your local Indian Dealer will be glad to tell you all about the Indian Scout-the greatest Motorcycle in the world, or write us for free descriptive literature and name of your nearest Indian Dealer". As an advertising card, this one is probably quite rare as it is the only one I have seen. It was originally printed in black and white, not the sepia tone that I have made it for this book.

107

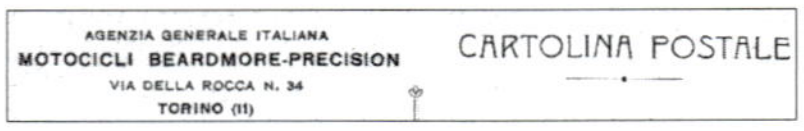

Beardmore-Precision motorcycles were built at Birmingham England between 1921 and 1924. The company was a merger of talents between F.E. Baker who built the Precision proprietary engine and the William Beardmore Steel Co. The gas tank was made to replace the top frame tube of the cycle and leaf spring suspension was used.

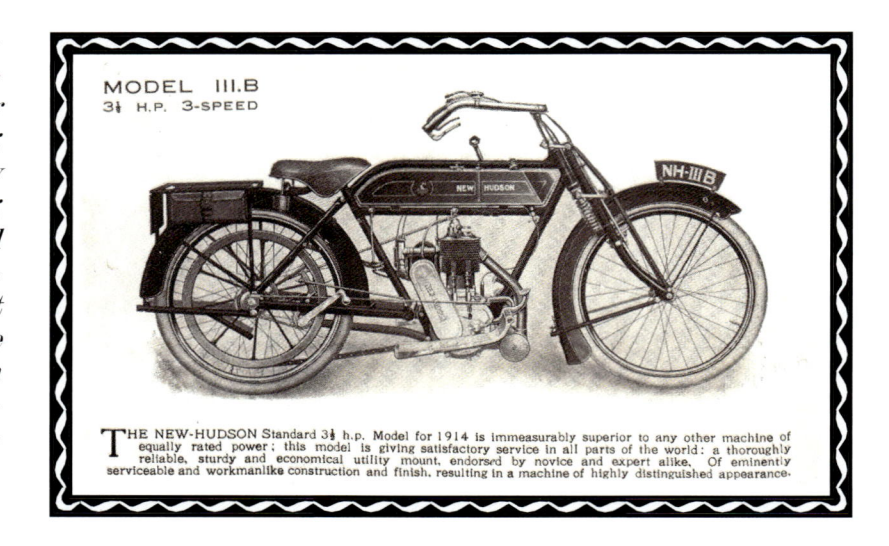

"*The New-Hudson Standard 3-1/2 h.p. model for 1914 is immeasurably superior to any other machine of equally rated power; this model is giving satisfactory service in all parts of the world: a thoroughly reliable, sturdy and economical utility mount, endorsed by novice and expert alike. Of eminently serviceable and workmanlike construction and finish, resulting in a machine of highly distinguished appearance.*"

New Hudson motorcycles were built in England between 1909 and 1957. The card shown here is advertising the Model III.B, a 3-1/2 h.p., 3 speed which was the 1914 model that they claimed "*immeasurably superior to any other machine of equally rated power. This model is giving satisfactory service in all parts of the world.*"

CHAPTER VI:
HOLIDAYS

Motorcycling Through History

Here is a charming new year greeting, at least at first glance. The caption tells things a bit differently.

*"At home the kids are screaming
The wife has pain but you
Drive with a motorcycle woman
Laughing into the world"*

It is very hard to condone the sentiment expressed here although the open road does have a great allure when things at home are troubling.

Prosit Neujahr!

Zu Hause schrei'n die Kinder,
Die Frau hat Not und Pein,
Indessen fährst Du mit der Motorbraut,
Vergnügt in die Welt hinein!

In this image, the cyclist appears to be bringing his troubles with him although the caption indicates otherwise.

"Me and my doll do not care about anything".

It is obvious that this couple is entering the new year with an attitude of defiance and individualism. In today's culture, the sentiment would be enhanced with a raised middle finger.

Prosit Neujahr!

Mir und meiner Puppe —
Uns ist alles schnuppe!

Another Happy New Year greeting is shown here. The date on the cancel cannot be read, but the postmark itself is quite interesting.

Ein frohes Neues Jahr

110

Chapter VI: Holidays

This young Hungarian is out for a cold ride with his lucky pigs. The caption reads "Happy New Year". Posted 29 December 1941.

These two colorful Gnomes with their flowing white beards and mushroom hats are wishing us all a happy new year from Romania. Their greeting was posted on 21 December 1930.

2101

Here is another New Years greeting from Hungary. Lucky pigs, and four leaf clovers lend a charm to the approaching new year. The hand written date on this card is 28 December 1928. In spite of the pigs and clover, 1929 was anything but a lucky year.

301

111

Motorcycling Through History

There is certainly a lot of pork displayed in these two New Year greeting cards. These are obviously Harley riders. It seems that Ma, Pa and Piglet have found riches and four leaf clovers to see them happily into the new year. If they are truly lucky pigs, they may be on their way home from a visit to the casino.

W S+S B 8908

It is very possible that with the amount of pork shown here, these riders are American Congressional Representatives. They are heading home from a session of congress with hefty bags of money for their local pet projects. Not to worry, when they get back to Washington they can vote themselves a pay raise and slap each other on the back.

W S+S B 8908

Head uut aastat!

Head uut aastat!

"*Happy New Year*" "*Gone is the old year, with all the joy and sorrows, that the new year may bring you only beautiful things*". What a cheerful greeting for the new year. With their lucky horse shoe, and clovers, this happy couple seem delighted to be riding into another year.

Rolcat 1445

Gelukkig Nieuwjaar

Verdwenen is het oude jaar, met al de vreugd en zorgen. Dat in het nieuwe, voor U slechts 't mooie is geborgen.

112

Chapter VI: Holidays

Postkarte — Carte postale
Weltpostverein — Union postale universelle
Correspondenz-Karte — Dopisnice
Levelező-Lap — Korespondencni listek
Dopisnica — Karta korespondencyjna
Briefkaart — Cartolina Postale — Brefkort
Brevkort — Tarjeta Postal — Postcard
ОТКРЫТОЕ ПИСЬМО

One would expect this card to have a European postmark. It was actually posted to Illinois from Los Angeles in 1907. It is a divided back card noted to be series 240.

Post Card-Postkarte-Carte postale

Printed in Germany, this embossed card is E.C.C. Serie 19. It was posted from Evansville, Ind. On Dec. 24th 1912.

"A Happy New Year"

Happy New Year from Yugoslavia is the message carried by this young couple and their dog. The card was posted from Zagreb in 1937 and is Amag card No. 2996.

Amag

113

Motorcycling Through History

Another new year greets this happy couple. Coming from the Netherlands, and welcoming in the year 1941 is this delightful card, posted on Dec. 31st. 1940.

This Valentine card is nicely embossed so that the motorcycle is slightly raised above the card. It was not posted, but says: "From Wesley to Anna, Barnes, Kansas.

"Much luck in the new year" reads this card from Estonia. This happy but cold cyclist doesn't seem to care about the weather since he has his clover and lucky pig. The cancellation on the stamp appears to read 1938, Vohma Eesti.

114

Chapter VI: Holidays

Valentines Day is a special time for millions of people and postcards help to pass on greetings to family and friends. This card simply says: *"To Aunt Rhoda from Henrietta."*

Here is another highly embossed German postcard. It is most likely from ca. 1912 being nearly identical to the Happy New Year card shown elsewhere that was posted in that year. *"To Viola from Florence"* is all this card says. This card has a divided back and is No. 18. American valentine cards with motorcycles are not too common.

Technically this is not a Valentine card, but I wont' tell if you won't. Coming from the Netherlands, this card was posted in 1933 and has the following publishers information: "Uitg.: J. Sleding, Amsterdam." This is one of those unique postcards that has a window that opens up exposing a series of photo views. In this case the card says: *"Greetings from Nymegen."* The front of the sidecar lifts up to view the photo's inside.

115

Motorcycling Through History

There are all kinds of critters on motorcycles, but this pairing has to be among the most unusual. From the normal frog perspective, this passenger is just along for lunch. How this greeting, wishing us a "Happy Pentecost" relates to the characters is anyone's guess. The church in the background lends some credibility to the religious theme, but it still looks as though lunch is about to be served.

Here we see that our beetle friends survived without being eaten and are able to take time to celebrate the Pentecost holiday by bringing in a load of springtime Lilly-of-the-valley. Their cycle is an early German design that did not survive the rigors of harsh dirt roads. This card was postmarked in 1915, the same time frame as the card above it.

My apologizes for laying this card on it's side. It was that or leave it out of the book. It completes this page and allows me to show the marvelous postal cancel from 1935 when the card was mailed.

116

Chapter VI: Holidays

Veselé Velikonoce!

C. Kotyšan
1. dubna 1931

Důstojnému Pánu,

Příjemných velkonočních
svátků přejí a srdečně
pozdravují
Jaroslav Hošek,
správce školy
— v Žeravinách, —
p. Hroznová Lhota.
s rodinou.

Here is a happy couple out on a lovely spring, Easter Sunday. Mr. Rabbit has only one thought in mind, that being to save his hide from the approaching cycle. This is obviously not the Easter bunny or the riders would be showing more respect. "Happy Easter" reads the card. Amag 2729

Gelukkig Paaschfeest

For Christians, Easter is a joyous time and on a light hearted note the Easter Bunny pays a visit. At left we see the bunny and his friends off to make someone happy. This is an embossed card, printed in Germany and posted on April 14th 1911 to Milwaukee WI. Shown below is an identifying mark from the back of the card.

TRADE MARK
2141

117

Motorcycling Through History

From Estonia comes this cheerful Easter greeting.

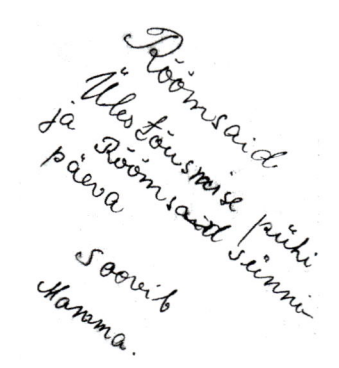

Coming from the Netherlands is this cute card. *"Happy Easter"* the card reads. Mr. Chicken and his load of colored eggs are no doubt off to please some children. This card was posted in 1933 from Deventer. The publishers mark below and an additional number 3541 appear on the back of this card.

It would be a reasonable guess to assume that this card is also celebrating the Easter holiday. Whereas in the card above where Mr. Chicken is delivering eggs, here we see the Easter Rabbit delivering his load of eggs. This card was posted to Budapest, Hungary, but a date is not available.

609

118

Chapter VI: Holidays

Here is another page of Easter greetings, all of which are from Germany. This one was drawn by the artist Hannes Petersen. Tied to the handle bars appears to be an egg large enough to have come from something prehistoric. The young lady has an egg that looks like it has been gift wrapped. Together the two eggs could amount to some rather large omelets.

HWB   SER.   5434

This Easter greeting was posted from Berlin on 10 April 1930.

W
S+S 1126
B   9860

Written in April of 1941 this beautiful card certainly is doing it's part to help celebrate the Easter holiday.

9383

119

Motorcycling Through History

A sidecar full of flowers brings lovely Easter greetings and the threat of a crushing death to the chicks in it's way. Somehow there is a mixed message here. Still this German card portrays a nice spring time greeting.

No 2054

Hannes Petersen is the artist on this German postcard. There are other examples of his work on various pages of this book. As a generic greeting card, this one could definitely fit the Easter category with it's springtime look.

EAS 7813

Here is another card that sparkles in the light with it's lovely gold embossed coloring. It is indeed a lovely Easter greeting with the Easter rabbit doing his best to bring a smile to all those he passes.

Rokat 1298

120

Chapter VI: Holidays

Here is another Easter greeting from Europe. This one was posted to Budapest late in the 1920s. These Easter bunnies are carrying their cargo of colored eggs while dressed in style and sounding a horn announcing their arrival.

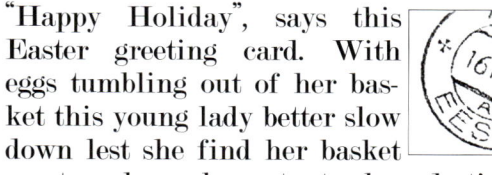

"Happy Holiday", says this Easter greeting card. With eggs tumbling out of her basket this young lady better slow down lest she find her basket empty when she gets to her destination. Posted from Estonia in 1938, this spring greeting card brings a happy message.

"Happy Easter"

These greetings come from Estonia. Our friend, the Easter Bunny is intent on getting his load of eggs to their destination. Apparently some of these eggs were not hard boiled, if the baby chicks have been shaken out of their shells. The sprig of pussy willow on the handle bars is another sign of Spring.

121

Motorcycling Through History

Below is another Easter card. This one was posted from Czechoslovakia on March 28, 1929. The card has a divided back and is another in the series by the publisher shown in the symbol below: The card is number 1679.

The bunny workers below are busy delivering colored eggs. The motorcycle makes for quick delivery in rural Germany where this card was posted. The date is not legible.

30 March 1931.

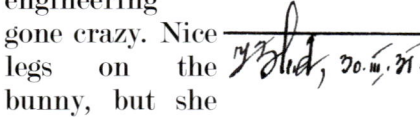

At right is an example of genetic engineering gone crazy. Nice legs on the bunny, but she is not playboy material. This card was printed in the Netherlands and posted in Yugoslavia.

W
S + S 8743 Import
B

122

Chapter VI: Holidays

As seen on the last few pages, Easter and motorcycles seem to go together especially from the Eastern European perspective. This card was posted from Nr. 4037 Czechoslovakia in 1935.

Happy Easter from Austria. What could be more traditional than The Easter Rabbit, chickens and Easter eggs. This image has it all.

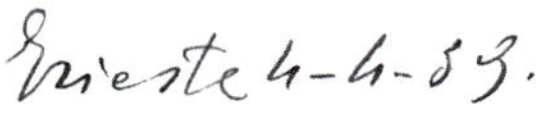

Veselé Velikonoce

Fröhliche Ostern

Buona Pasqua

This nice Italian Easter greeting was posted from Trieste on 4 April in what looks like 1933. The card reads *"Happy Easter"*.

123

Motorcycling Through History

From Belgium comes this happy Easter chicken. Probably dating from the 1930s, this card portrays another joyous Easter greeting. With one hand steering and one on the horn, Mr. Chicken and his powerful motorcycle are destined to deliver a load of eggs on time for the holiday.

M. 1416

26 March 1937. "Happy Easter" from Yugoslavia. This card was posted to Zagreb, a city in what is now Croatia. Slightly embossed and with an especially shiny, bright surface this Easter greeting with it's sidecar egg is very charming.

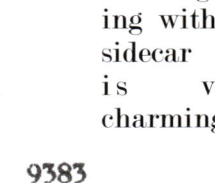

9383

Easter greetings are once again depicted in this cute card. This bunny couple appears on another card in this section. Both cards are from the Netherlands, but posted from Yugoslavia. Momma bunny seems to be having quite a problem keeping her eggs in the basket or is papa just hitting every bump in sight. Sidecars can be a bit bumpy.

W S+S 8743 B

124

Chapter VI: Holidays

On this page are another group of cards celebrating the Easter season. Translated from Dutch, this card says *"Happy Easter"*. The card was posted in Belgium, but the date is not legible. It has a plain divided back with the publishers symbol shown below.

EAS 1274

This is a variation on the Dutch card shown above. This one is Finish. It was posted on April 18, 1935. It has a divided back that says *"Carte Postale"* but no other identifying marks are shown. The card above and this one are essentially the same card except for the chicken in the sidecar which has been replaced by a pretty young lady. The card reads: *"Happy Spring Holidays"*.

This cute chicken family is traveling through the province of Bohemia which was located ESE of Prague in the Czech Republic. The card was posted on April 4th 1941 from Tschaslau, Caslay. The dividing line on this card says *"printed in Czechoslovakia"*. Other than that information, there is a number 7688-2 and it says *"import"*. The theme of this card is very much like the ones above to include freshly painted Easter eggs.

125

Motorcycling Through History

Below is one of Santa's Eastern European helpers. This is Bonzo, a popular cartoon character. He is loaded down with presents and a nice Christmas tree to brighten someone's parlor.

W S + S 8369 B

BREVKORT

"Merry Christmas" says this Danish Santa. His racing stripe pants seem a bit odd compared to other Santa's seen in this book.

Konstbilaga för Mors Julbrev av Erik O. Strandman.

Here is yet another Christmas greeting probably from the late 1920s to early 1930s. This card may also be from Denmark as is the card shown above. This one has been addressed to Falkoping, a town in southern Sweden. Santa postcards are highly desirable and to many collectors they are collected for the variety of colors that Santa wears in his coat.

Ed. F. Ph. Eneret Nr. 2637

126

Chapter VI: Holidays

The image of Santa shown below is especially beautiful and typical of a lot of the early German cards. This card was not posted although it had a handwritten message in German. This card probably dates before 1910.

"Joyeux Noel" says Santa as he delivers his load of gifts throughout the French countryside. Posted to an address in France, this is a plain divided back postcard with a simple message "Bon Noel a natre petite Gante Galice. Ceci Pette"

Look at the loving smile on Santa as he peers down upon the Sweet little angel. the year is no longer on the cancel because the stamp was removed, but it is obvious that this greeting was sent on December 23. This is an especially lovely card that is fairly rare.

127

Motorcycling Through History

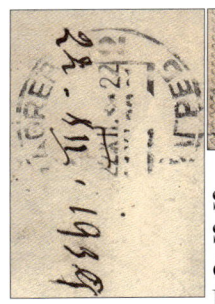

So who says that Santa needs Rudolph and a bunch of reindeer to fly? Not is Yugoslavia. Santa is flying high here with Krampus poking out of his bag. With a little wind at his back Santa's sidecar rig should arrive in plenty of time for Christmas.

At right is a divided back card that was not posted but bears the following message: "Malta, Xmas 1928. With love to Marjorie from Auntie Nana, Uncle John, & Emil. Happy Xmas". This card was printed in Germany and has this identifying mark on the reverse.

What is more traditional at Christmas time than angels? Most of us do not associate angels with motorcycles, but however the message is delivered, it helps bring the true meaning of Christmas to the forefront. This card was posted in Hungary on 23 Dec. 1924, just in time for the holiday.

220

128

Chapter VI: Holidays

Here is a nice Santa card with a rear facing passenger car. The card was posted from Hackley, Wisconsin on Dec. 7, 1910. This card as well as the one below are from the same printing company although it is not identified. Both are embossed cards with a capital A in a circle. This card is No. 708-1 from the series. The Santa cards on ths page are fairly common.

This card bears the writing, *"Leland from Mamma"*. A more traditional sidecar arrangement is shown. This card is numbered 708-4. The back is distinctive. An identical card to this one was posted on 12-22-1909 to Washington State.

"Merry Christmas", states this postcard from Yugoslavia. Posted just after Christmas in 1938 this happy card has Santa and his helpers off to please the waiting children. With presents and a basket of apples, Mr. Claus is sure to bring smiles.

129

Motorcycling Through History

Posted on 20 Dec. 1929 this lovely card was published in the Netherlands, posted in Austria and mailed to Paris. Santa is delivering a Teddy bear, doll, rocking horse, ball, drum and tennis racket. Not a bad load for under the tree. This is a fairly available card.

W
S+S 8157 Import
B

Here is an extremely early and rare Santa postcard. It is from France, but bears no postmark. It probably dates from the first few years of the last century. Trailers like the one shown were popular at that time. The subtle colors of this card make it especially attractive.

B|D   107

The card shown here is very similar to the one on the previous page with slight variations. The stars in the background are much more prominent and the color tones are somewhat different. Although the Christmas wish is basically the same, the message is slightly different. This card was addressed to Clinton, Ohio but was never posted. It is heavily embossed. Variations of this card are widely available.

Chapter VI: Holidays

The Christmas holidays often brought Santa out on his motorcycle. This is a nicely embossed German card that was posted from, and to Cleveland, Ohio on Christmas Day, 1909. This lovely card has Santa riding an early forecar style motorcycle that had an up-front passenger seat made of wicker. The earliest types of sidecars and forecars as well as trailers were made of wicker. This is a very common card but still desirable.

Perhaps more people are familiar with sidecars than forecars. This example shows Santa and his happy young passenger bundled up for a ride through the snow. It was not than many years earlier that this scene would have been with a horse and buggy. This is another nicely embossed German card that has printed on the back: B.W. 324 Printed in Germany. A simple message says "Lilly from Granny." The card shown here and the one below are also fairly common.

Coming from the Netherlands is this card, posted to Rotterdam on Dec. 19, 1916. The text on the front of this card reads, "Happy Christmas." It is a divided back card that has the symbol shown above in the stamp box.

131

Motorcycling Through History

This green suited Santa with his bag of goodies is riding off through the snow to carry the "Happy Christmas" greeting. The only information from this card is the written message shown below. This card is fairly unusual and uncommon.

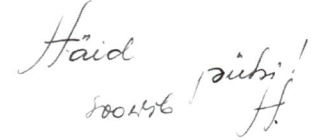

The postmark on this card is a little late for Christmas, but it is the thought that counts. The card was posted from Finland on Dec. 31, 1917 and wishes us a Merry Christmas.

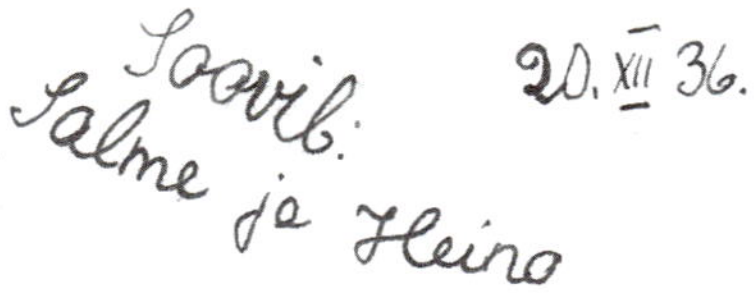

Santa and his helper better be careful lest they lose more of their Christmas packages. This card most likely originated in Estonia.

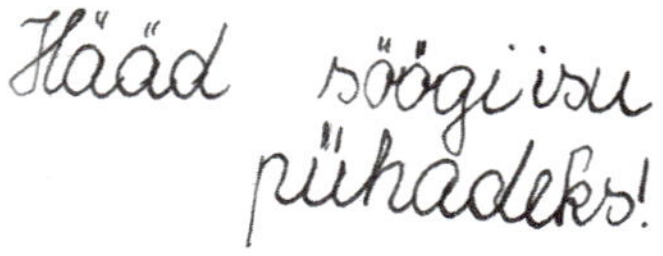

Chapter VI: Holidays

The only identifying information on this card is the name of the presumed artist shown below and the date which is later than most cards in this book. The card does fit in well with those on this and the next page which portray Santa and or Krampus. Both are symbols of the holiday season pairing the good with the bad. Krampus cards are common in Eastern Europe.

A. Stefsky, Wien IX 47

Posted December 4th 1909 from Austria, this is an especially nice, early Santa and Krampus card.

"St. Nicholas is being modern, that goes without question. On the motorcycle also sits behind him a devil."

C. H. W. VIII/2. 2505-31

The hairy fellow in this image is not about to let his prize get away. Chained to Krampus, the young lady seems to have resigned herself to her fate. This card may date from the 1920s.

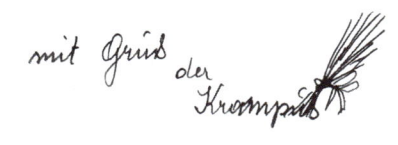

mit Gruß der Krampus

BR& 3996

133

Motorcycling Through History

Here is the team of Krampus and St. Nikolaus. The devil looking creature is Krampus whose task is to take the evil children and put them in his large sack. St. Nikalous represents good and Krampus evil. The tradition of Krampus is particularly strong in Austria.

Below we see Krampus riding off with an unfortunate young lady. If she is paying for being evil, her sweet look might suggest that she has been wrongly accused. It would not be the first time that a fair maiden was punished wrongly by puritanical zealots. This card and the one to it's left are quite common.

Here is another card depicting Santa's arch rival, Krampus. Often they can be found together, but this image has the horned one out terrorizing a very frightened passenger. Perhaps the gentleman is being made to atone for past sins. This card was posted from Romania in what looks like 1933. As a Krampus postcard, this one is very uncommon and desirable.

134

Chapter VI: Holidays

Very heavily embossed, this lovely German greeting card was posted on December 21, 1910 as a Christmas and New Year greeting from a secret admirer. It reads *"from a friend"* to Clifford.

At left is a divided back card posted from Marietta, Ohio on Nov. 10, 1911. The generic nature of this card would make it suitable for many types of greetings. The floral decorations make this an especially attractive card.

This lovely card, like the one above was printed in Germany. It is identified as the "G.-A. NOVELTY ART SERIES No. 1268 (Relief) (6 Des.) printed in Germany. It is an embossed card and expresses a generic greeting. This card was posted from Hayton, Wisconsin on Feb. 20, 1909.

Motorcycling Through History

"Happy Birthday" These greetings come to us from Estonia. This young couple is on their way to deliver that message to some special person. Mustla, is the name of the city that this card was posted from in 1940.

Printed in Germany, this beautiful birthday greeting is highlighted in gold which is brilliant in the way it stands out above the surface of the card. Greeting type postcards do not get much lovelier than this.

HWB SER. 1281

The wings of this moth hold an image of remarkable clarity. As a postcard, this is one of the most unusual to be seen. It is heavily embossed with an especially glossy finish. The scene, with wicker sidecar is from the early teens of the 1900s. The colors are brilliant. In the left wing of the moth are found the Numbers 7385.D and in the right wing is Rotary Photo E.C. An unusual and rare card.

136

Chapter VI: Holidays

Birthdays are an occasion long celebrated and postcard publishers did not miss printing cards to celebrate the events. The card at left was posted from Berrien Springs, Michigan on Feb. 7th in what looks like 1908. It is a nicely embossed card, Ser. 240. It is a bit of a stretch to view this as a motorcycle, but some creative artist seems to have had a unique ideas of how a cycle should be powered. In actuality some machines were built with the engine as part of the front wheel.

Postkarte — Carte postale
Weltpostverein — Union postale universelle
Correspondenz- Karte — Dopisnice —
Levelező- Lap   Korespondencni listek
Dopisnica — Karta korespondencyjna
Briefkaart — Cartolina Postale — Brefkort
Brevkort   Tarjeta Postal — Postcard
ОТКРЫТОЕ ПИСЬМО

Another heavily embossed card in subtle color is this German card. It has the No. 72 on the back and a divided back. It simply reads *"From Leon To Anna"*. The German cards are among some of the loveliest of postcards.

Post Card— Postkarte— Carte postale

Who would not be happy to receive such a beautiful birthday card as this one? Although this card was not posted perhaps it found it's intended recipient. Heavily embossed and beautifully colored, this card most likely dates from around 1910. The paper of this card is unusually thin and especially glossy unlike other similar cards shown.

137

Motorcycling Through History

This "Charlie Chaplin" looking fellow is having quite a problem and would be well advised to seek out a better trailer for his merchandise. With presents, wine and flowers, this has all the makings for a fine birthday party.

"From whole heart, congratulations for your birthday"

W S+S 1126 B

Auch ich gratuliere herzlich zum Geburtstag!

"From whole heart, congratulations for your birthday"
This must be the female version of the above card, meant to be sent to male friends. Do you suppose that it means anything that this wagon is missing the bottle of wine". The card was posted in March of 1928.   W S+S 1126 B

Auch ich gratuliere herzlich zum Geburtstag!

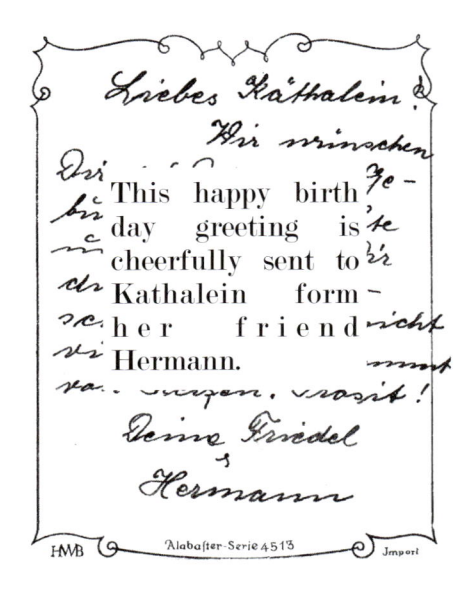

This happy birthday greeting is cheerfully sent to Kathalein form her friend Hermann.

Herzlichen Glückwunsch zum Geburtstage

138

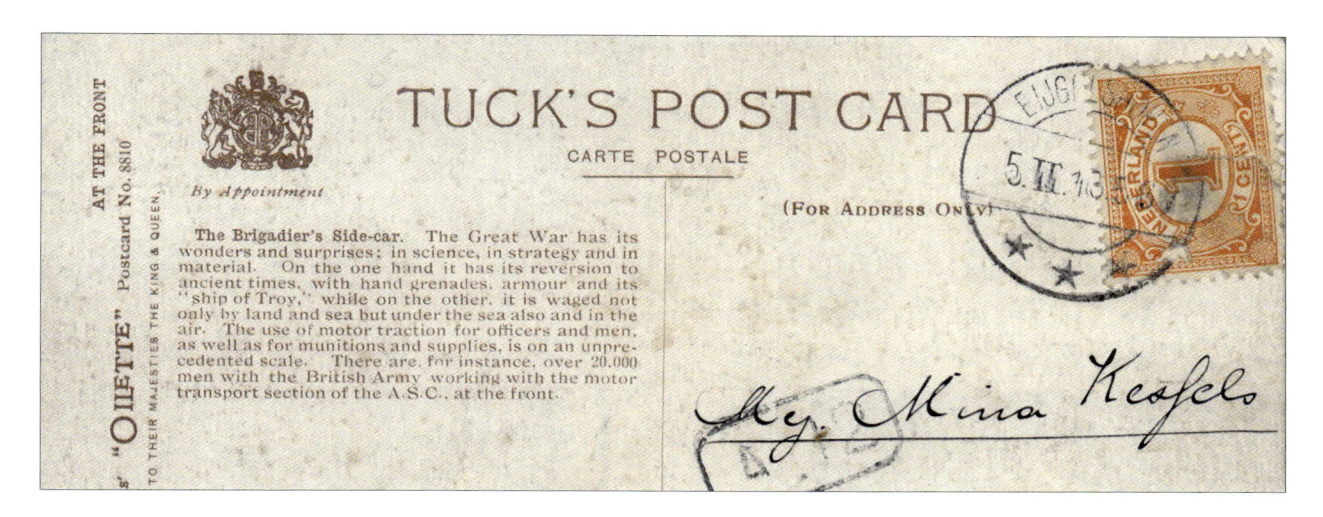

TUCK'S POST CARD
CARTE POSTALE

By Appointment

AT THE FRONT
"OILETTE" Postcard No. 8810
TO THEIR MAJESTIES THE KING & QUEEN.

The Brigadier's Side-car. The Great War has its wonders and surprises; in science, in strategy and in material. On the one hand it has its reversion to ancient times, with hand grenades, armour and its "ship of Troy," while on the other, it is waged not only by land and sea but under the sea also and in the air. The use of motor traction for officers and men, as well as for munitions and supplies, is on an unprecedented scale. There are, for instance, over 20,000 men with the British Army working with the motor transport section of the A.S.C., at the front.

(For Address Only)

CHAPTER VII: MILITARY

139

Motorcycling Through History

The photo below reads: "Mobilisatic 1914". The photograph appears to have been taken in a studio, a setting that was commonly used. This motorcycle is a beautiful ca. 1914 Royal Enfield. The Enfield Manufacturing Co. was founded in 1893 near Redditch, England.

This photo shows a WWI era Triumph motorcycle. It could be a ca. 1915 model H which had a 550cc engine. The happy looking British soldier has sent this card *"To my big sister Mary, with love, Charley."* One has to wonder if Charlie survived the Great War where so many perished.

Here is a remarkable sidecar rig. It's happy crew are sitting on a Campion cycle which was produced at Nottingham, England between 1901 and 1926. This model probably dates from pre-WWI. The sidecar is especially unique in it's design, not so much for the wicker, but for the bullet shape which became a common design in steel. This card has not been posted and is of the divided back style.

Chapter VII: Military

Shown below is an image titled "The Brigadier's Side Car." The artist signed card gives credit to "Oilette." This is a "Tucks Post Card", one of the great publishers of early post cards. There is a lot of information on this card as shown on the chapter heading page. Posted from the Netherlands, the date is not entirely legible. A good assumption puts the date prior to 1912.

This nice image is of a French Army motorcyclist. The style of the motorcycle probably represents a WWI era type H Terrot. This card is signed "Paul Barbier-40". It is possible that the painting was done in 1940 but the subject seems definitely earlier. The card has a plain divided back and is printed "Editions d'Art— Andre Leconte, 38 rue Sainte-Croix-de-la-Bretonnerie, Paris. Fabrication Francaise– Reproduction Interdite".

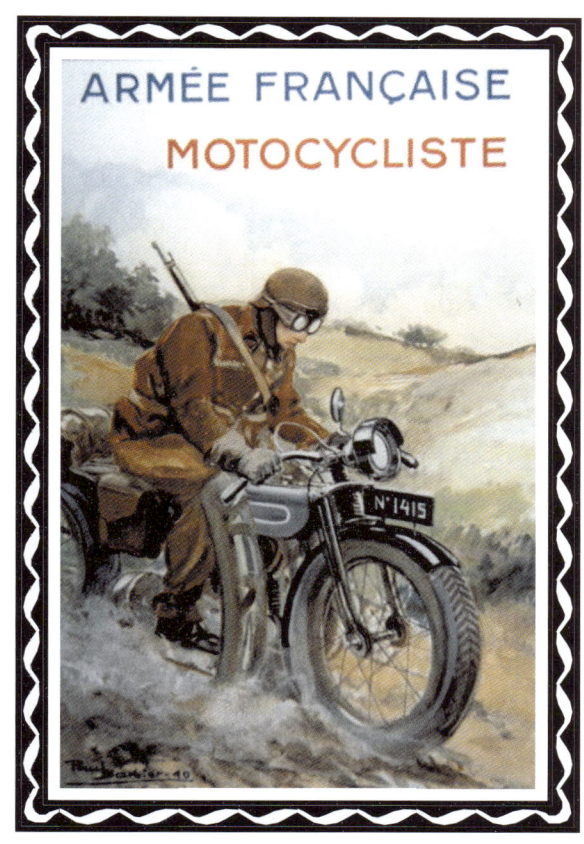

CARTE POSTALE
Fusil-mitrailleur contre avion.

The French soldiers shown here are using their heavy duty Rene-Gillet sidecar combination as a battlefield weapon. These machines were used by both the military and police. This machine is probably a type G, 750cc model from the late 1920s to the mid to late 1930s.

GEORGES LANG, Imp. - Paris

141

Motorcycling Through History

Photo's of early BMW cycles on postcards are quite uncommon and hard to find in the U.S.A. This appears to be a German soldier leaning on his ca. 1927-1928, machine. BMW introduced it's first motorcycle in 1923, known as the R32 model. Over the last eighty years, BMW has retained it's distinctive "Boxer" engine and shaft drive. Know for their outstanding quality and reliability, BMW cycles have a loyal following.

Riding what is probably a German Triumph ca. 1938 are these two smiling Nazi soldiers. This photo was posted from Nuremberg on Dec. 13, 1938. The sidecar is the Steib S501 distinctive with It's classic bullet nose styling. Germany began building Triumphs in 1903 as a part of the British Triumph Co. of Coventry. Siegfried Betman headed up the German operation which was located in Nuremberg. A message on the back ends in "Heil Hitler".

Shown here is another German motorcycle. In all likelihood this is a model K800 Zundapp which was a favorite of the Wehrmacht. It had a four cylinder opposed engine that was ideally suited for tough sidecar use. This card was posted from Eisenach on Dec. 5, 1936. It is series Nr. 36/81 "Wehrmacht– u. luftwaffe Foto-Karten Veilag Hor... Gotha." Caption reads: "Schreibt u, sammelt ,, Horns" ech.. Foto Karten sie bereiten Freude.

142

Chapter VII: Military

The card at left shows a group of Belgian motorcyclists and a bicyclist. The motorcycles have 4 cylinder, inline engines and are probably the FN made in Belgium. These cycles had shaft drives with engine displacements of 496cc and 748cc. Many of these machines were built for the Army. This image from 1914 – 1915 was probably taken at Oostende, a seaport in West Flanders Province, N.W. Belgium. In 1914 the Germans seized the port for a submarine base.

What a superbly sharp photo this is. It is a great example of German military personnel from 1937. This team hauling a machine gun is riding a Zundapp motorcycle, which was heavily used by the Germans especially for sidecar use because of it's heavy frame and powerful engine.

At left is a very nice image of pre-WW1 military in Hungary. The two cycles shown are a Wanderer in the foreground and behind it is a Puch with a sidecar. Both of these cycles are very early machines. The card appears to be postmarked 9 Feb. 1910. The Wanderer was made in Germany beginning in 1902 whereas the Puch was made in Austria as early as 1903.

57 Magy. Fenynyomdai Részv.-Tars. Bpest

Motorcycling Through History

CARTE POSTALE

The three cards on this page depict aspects of the war in France, with motorcycles as a focal point. None of the cards have been posted or bear any date other than as stated on the fronts of the cards. This one, No. 1503 in the series is dated 1917 and shows English soldiers surveying the damage at Peronne, a town on the Somme River, 35 miles N. E. of Amiens.

The card to the right shows the devastating effects of the war at Romagne-sous-Montfaucon, France. Near this town in N.E. France is the site of the largest American military cemetery in France holding the graves of over 14,000 soldiers. The front, bottom right of the card reads: M. Bertrand, elit. Lyon-Depose. On the back lower left corner is the following symbol:

CARTE POSTALE

At right is a scene showing the effects of the bombing at Verdun between 1914 and 1916. Located in N.E. France on the Meuse river, Verdun was the site of massive resistance by the French against the Germans. Nearly a million soldiers died there. The image is No. 1464 and published by (ELD), E. LE DEDLEY, PARIS.

144

Chapter VII: Military

To the left are two English motorcyclists riding Douglas cycles into France. This image pre-dates WWI as noted by the printed dates on the card. The card reads as follows: "242 Guerre de 1914-15. Motocyclistes anglais, porteurs d'ordres, renseignes par une sentinelle francaise". This card was printed by G. Mathiere, 34 rue de Charonne, Paris. The French sentinel is giving directions to the Englishmen. The fore-aft horizontal twin engines are distinctive in the Douglas motorcycle.

As shown in the card above, this card was also printed in France. "ANCIENS ETAB. NEURDEIN ET CIE.— IMP. CRETE, SUCC, CORBEIL-PARIS. 52, AV. DE BRETEUIL.— PARIS." This is a nice image described as a "kitchen in a base of revictualling. In the foreground is a nice Indian sidecar rig. It appears to be a ca. 1917 powerplus model. Meals for these American soldiers, and life in general was not very appealing.

In terms of detail and dramatic interest this WWI artist drawn image is quite spectacular. The French motorcycle courier has blasted his way through six German soldiers without being hit in return. That is a pretty amazing feat, straight out of someone's imagination.

Galerie Patriotique - (visé Paris N° au verso)
A. Noyer, Imp., Edit., 22, rue Ravignan, Paris

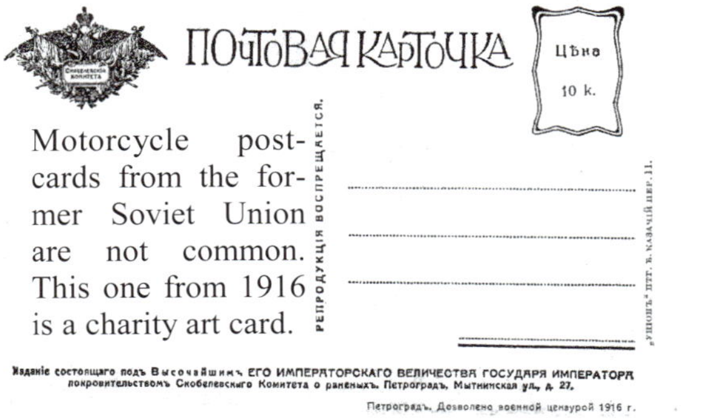

Motorcycling Through History

Motorcycle postcards from the former Soviet Union are not common. This one from 1916 is a charity art card.

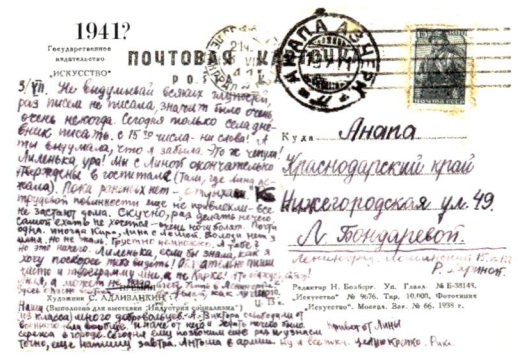

The riders in this photo are identified as Lieut. Blancu, on the left and Joe and Riley on the right. It is assumed that the driver of the left rig is George, the sender of the card writing to his friend, Jessie. He complains that it is cold but the roads are still fine for driving.

146

Chapter VII: Military

INDIAN TROOPS LYNDHURST

POST CARD BRITISH MADE.
Correspondence | Address

It is believed the motorcycle shown here is the British made N.U.T. The initials stand for Newcastle Upon Tyne where the machine was made. This image is from the early 1920s at Lyndhurst, England. N.U.T. motorcycles were built with V-twin engines notably the JAP, but also from their own manufacture. The N.U.T. is a very uncommon image to find on a postcard.

K. C. HUT, VLADIVOSTOK, OCTOBER, 1919

This is a rare postcard with divided back that was not posted or written on. A simple printing on the reverse says <u>SOLDIERS MAIL</u> A. E. F., SIBERIA. This photo was taken in front of the Knights of Columbus Hut in Vladivostok, Russia, in October of 1919. Serving in Russia at that time was the "Polar Bear" Division of the U.S. Army. They were a tough bunch of soldiers having been forced to fight under some of the most adverse weather conditions.

ARMÉE ANGLAISE. — Messager motocycliste.

Carte Postale
Correspondance | Adresse

Seen here are a group of British soldiers in Belgium or France. The motorcycle looks to be a Belgium FN, single cylinder machine. This example could be from around 1910-1915. The engine was a 2-1/2 H.P. model that was air cooled and mounted transversely in the frame. It could manage 20 mph., getting around 75 miles per gallon.

147

Motorcycling Through History

This U.S. infantryman, a.k.a. doughboy of WWI, sits astride his Harley-Davidson sidecar rig. This nice sepia portrait is on the front of an AZO postcard that was never mailed or written on. The faded out edges of this photo make it quite unusual. In WWI, motorcycles were a very important part of the U.S. military and Harley and Indian both provided machines to support the war effort. They served as transportation, carried medical stretchers, machine guns, and hauled materials.

What seems apparent in this photo is that it was probably taken at the same place as the one above. The studio backdrop seems the same as does the motorcycle. The mule adds a special touch to this photo as a reminder that in WWI not everything was as mechanized as in later years. The stamp box on this card is a relatively uncommon one.

This is a French made postcard the words "CARTE POSTALE" printed at the top center of the back. Having never been posted, nothing is known of the two soldiers pictured. They are U.S. soldiers on their Harley-Davidson rig. This Harley is probably ca. 1916-1918. This would have been a great photographic image to send back to family or friends. Only one word appears in the address line and that is Lucy. One wonders if she ever got the card or her man back.

148

Chapter VII: Military

To the left is a French postcard with the number 237 and printed in Paris. It has an unusual hand stamped advertisement for boot polish on the rear. The painting is credited to H. Beorts and titled L'Heroism du Cycliste Maillet. (French Army soldier being chased by German horse patrol).

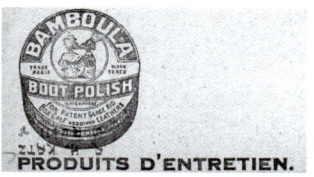

Shown here is an interesting card that was printed in England by Gale & Polden, Ltd. London, Aldershot, and Portsmouth. It is printed in English and Russian, reading: *"Forward comrades! Forward, friends!, Let us struggle on undaunted-struggle on till death in the name of Christ and Truth. From your friend, soldier of the Third Division. Christ is Risen!"*

This divided back card was never posted. The image definitely appears to be from the era of WWI. The nice colors make this an especially attractive card. The translation reads:

"On my bike I cross the meadows and the roads. while I am always thinking of you my dear. Don't think I will ever forget you."

149

Motorcycling Through History

At right is the stamp box for the first two cards on this page, both from the WWI era. They have nice color and sharp detail. Both were published by the Illustrated Postal Card & Nov. Co. N.Y.. This one is No. 1361-23. The caption reads: "*Motorcycle Scouts in action*" and shows a traditional sidecar pulled by an Indian motorcycle.

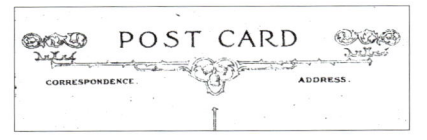

This is another Indian motorcycle with a machine gun sidecar attached. These vehicles served very well in many different areas and conditions. They were very maneuverable and could handle off road conditions quite easily. Often the difference between off-road and on-road was very little.

"*Armored Motor Cycle Machine Gun*"

Here is an obvious off-road situation with soldiers taking up positions behind a stone wall. This is another card that has not been posted. It is a divided back card published by H.H. Stratton, Chattanooga, Tenn.

"*The Motor Cycle Squad*"

Chapter VII: Military

The three WWI era cards on this page were all published by the same company, C.T. American Art. This particular card shows a Harley-Davidson set up for machine gun duty. The photo is by R. Runyon and says *"U.S. Motorcycle corps, showing armored motorcycle with machine gun"*.

This card was posted on Jul. 24, 1918 from San Diego to N. Dakota. It is titled *"Motorcycle Corps, U.S. Army"*. Most of the military cards in this series are very common and regularly offered on auction sites. Their value is not high.

This card shows the Medical Corps of the U.S. National Guard, Camp Sheridan, Montgomery, Alabama. It is an interesting choice of cards for the sender to have chosen to post to his Miss Helen, perhaps prophetic. He writes *"Am way down South and enjoying life in spite of the "flu". Please write to me soon. Best Love."*

151

Motorcycling Through History

The card shown here is a C.T. American Art card and says U.S. Army Cantonment series No. 79. This is an image of a Harley-Davidson with U.S. Army dispatch riders.

This card and the one below have the same back as the one above except there is no center dividing line that says C.T. American Art. This card says "pub. By Diehl Office Equipment Co. Columbus, Ohio." It shows Dispatch Riders, Camp Sherman, Chillicothe, Ohio.

Shown here are motorcycle gunners. The information on this card says that it is No. 104— Active Army Life— 26 Des. On the front it says "*Copy Press ILL Service Inc.*" Motorcycles were put to many diverse uses by the military. They were maneuverable, could work in many off-road conditions, and whether paired with a machine gun or stretcher they were highly regarded.

152

Chapter VII: Military

These Canadian soldiers are moving out for a hard days work with a Ca. 1913 P&M cycle. Looking at this crew, one has to wonder how much real work is going to be done. The P&M, for Phelon & Moore Ltd. was located at Cleckheaton, Yorkshire, England. They were a long lived motorcycle company with beginnings in the late 1800s and continuing into the 1960s.

Here is another group of Canadian soldiers. The photo says: *"Our Canadian troops, a few of the motorcycle squad with Canadian Signal Services"*. The soldiers are riding Indian motorcycles that date from around 1915.

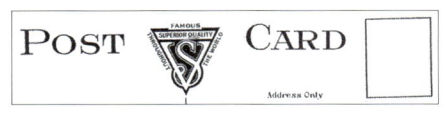

"Machine gun on motorcycle" This card was published by the Valentine-Souvenir Co., New York. Printed in the U.S.A. The photo is by Underwood & Underwood, N.Y. This Indian motorcycle has an interesting feature with the stabilizing rods from the handle bars to front wheel. It must have made for easier handling with the sidecar.

153

Motorcycling Through History

"Motor Cycle Machine Gun"
This is card No. 17 published by American Colortype Co., Chicago. A nice description is given as follows: *"The lightest thing in light, mobile artillery! As a matter of fact it is not considered artillery, but merely part of the up-to-date infantry equipment. This outfit can get around most anywhere and get there quick. The motorcycle is as handy and effective as a means of transportation as the machine gun is a weapon and the combination of the two constitutes a fighting machine which will make itself felt wherever there's an enemy to be fought. The United States Government has a large number of these machines all equipped and men trained to drive and operate them."*

"Motor Cycle Ambulance"
Another practical use for the motorcycle was as an evacuation unit for the wounded. It could easily travel to the front where the action and injured were found. This Indian motorcycle set up with stretcher enabled relatively quick, but probably very bumpy transportation back to the medics. This card is Series 575 Army-24 des. and copyright by Underwood & Underwood, N. Y.

"Motor-Cycle Brigade, Camp Dodge, Iowa"

Here is a group of Harley-Davidson motorcycles ready for action. The card itself, has not been posted and was published by Enos B. Hunt. I wonder if these soldiers thought as highly of their rigs on a cold, snowy morning as they do sitting here in the sunshine.

Chapter VII: Military

The reverse of this card says only *"Camp Harris, Macon, GA, 1917"* and is written in pencil. That date could be correct, but the cycles are older than that. In the background is an early Harley-Davidson and in the foreground is a ca. 1910-1911 Excelsior Auto Cycle. These soldiers look more like "rough riders" than "doughboys".

Here is a terrific, real photo card of early 20th century military hardware. The Indian that this machine gun is attached to was probably built around 1916 and was at the forefront of Indian's commitment to military production, while it put domestic production on hold. This was a decision that allowed Harley-Davidson to gain a large market share.

There is no date to help with this photo, but it is certainly in the era of WWI. These soldiers are posed in their Harley rigs, probably around 1918-1919. The image is very sharp and would be perfect if the individuals could be identified.

155

Motorcycling Through History

The message on this card is dated 1940, but the card was made in 1938 as the front shows. These are French soldiers and if one looks carefully, the French flag can be seen on the License plate.

Looking smug is this WWI era British soldier on his BSA. This could be a model "D", 3-1/2 H.P. machine with direct belt drive. A similar looking machine, the 4-1/4 H.P. model "H" was also built during WWI but it was an all chain drive unit. Still, a third model the "K" was also a 4-1/4 H.P. model, but this one had a belt final drive claimed to be particularly unsuited to the mud of Flanders.

Another WWI era British soldier is shown here on his Douglas, sidecar rig. This machine could be the 348 cc model with side valve, flat twin engine. A larger machine of 498 cc displacement was made and would have been better for sidecar use although the majority of machines supplied to the military during the first war were the 348 cc models. Douglas motorcycles were built between 1907 & 1956.

156

Chapter VII: Military

It is guessing time with this photograph. The motorcycle is quite an early example of a single cylinder, belt driven machine. It may date from as early as 1901 or 1902 and has characteristics of the French made Werner that was created by two Russian brothers who were living in Paris. The cycle carried their name for the years it was produced beginning in 1897 and ending in 1908.

The Simplex motorcycle was produced in Holland from 1902-1968. The earlier machines used a variety of engines including, Fafnir, Minerva and MAG. In the 1920s Blackburne, Bradshaw, and Villiers engines were also used. This is a great and unusual picture of a long lived motorcycle.

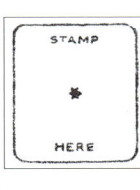

These young soldiers are sitting on identical machines with consecutively numbered plates. The motorcycles appear to be the British made P & M. They probably date from 1912-1913. At that time the 500cc P & M was chosen by the Royal Air Force to be it's standard machine. Note the cases of Mobil oil stacked next to the garage.

157

Motorcycling Through History

BSA was one of many motorcycle manufacturers supplying machines to their soldiers during WWI. This model was used widely by the British. The BSA insignia on the tank has been painted over designating this machine as part of the "Signals" corp. This cycle maintained it's belt drive although chain drives were also being produced by BSA. Slippage of the belt became a problem in the mud found at many battle fronts.

The soldier shown here riding an early 1920s BSA. is probably Bulgarian. A written date shows it as 25 May, 1926 and the location, Sofia. The BSA. Co. (Birmingham Small Arms) was founded in 1861 as a manufacturer of guns. By 1880 they were making bicycles and then around 1904 engines began to appear on their bicycle frames. It wasn't until 1910 that production motorcycles made their entry. 1972 was the last year of production.

This photograph and the one above appear as though they have been taken on the same motorcycle at the same location in Bulgaria. The written date on this one is three months later than the one above and the soldiers are different. One wonders how many soldiers posed for this photo and sent copies home to loved ones. What seems strange in both of these photo's is the lack of numbers on the number plate. In it's place is the identifying B.S.A. designation.

158

Chapter VII: Military

POST CARD

"*Motorcycle Couriers in action at Camp Gordon, GA.*"

Here are a pair of WWII Harley WLA models. Note the brackets on the front fender used for holding the rifle scabbard.

Published by Standard Paper Co. Augusta, Ga.

This WWII era card was published by the Chattanooga Magazine Co. Made in U.S.A. by E.C. Kropp Co., Milwaukee, Wis.

Of great historic interest is Chickamauga Park, a 5,565 acre Government park where the Chickamauga Battlefields are located. These Battlefields, which are kept in a natural state, still contain buildings which were used as hospitals and headquarters during the Civil War. Many monuments and markers, some noted for their beauty and size, have been erected here such as Wilder's Monument.

POST CARD

Here is a photo by Acme, No. 48171 that portrays the vulnerability of motorcycle troops when attacked.

159

Motorcycling Through History

The "Tommie" or British soldier and his French Guide. Do you think that his mind is on the war? This soldier has nicely mixed business with pleasure.

Imprimé en Belgique

LE TOMMIES ET SON GUIDE
DE TOMMIE EN ZIJN GIDS
THE TOMMIE AND IS GUIDE

Now the "Tommie" appears on course, carrying the Allied message that the Germans will be crushed.

Imprimé en Belgique

CE QUI EN ARRIVE
WAT ER VAN KOMT
WHAT COMES AT LAST

When it came to fighting the "great war", Harley-Davidson was generally part of the action. This rig is typical of WWI machines.

PLACE POSTAGE STAMP HERE

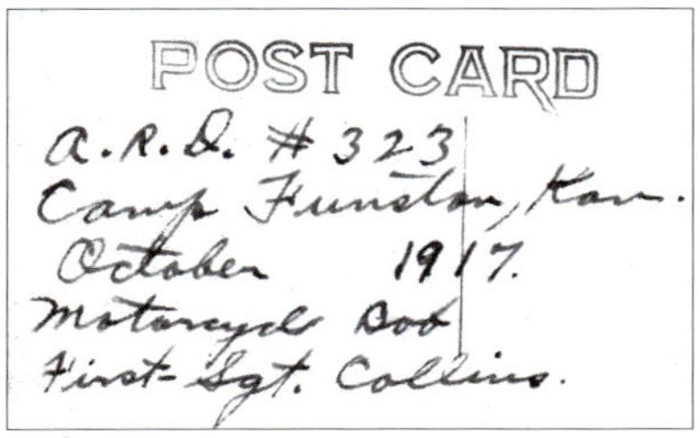

POST CARD
A.R.D. #323
Camp Funston, Kan.
October 1917.
Motorcycle Bob
First Sgt. Collins.

160

Chapter VII: Military

Left *"In my steel charger there is less fire than I have for you in the depths of my soul"*

Above *"Right near you, my poor heart beats louder than the motor on my motorcycle"*

Left *"I burn the pavement, drive like a daredevil to be able to stay longer near you."*

161

Motorcycling Through History

Right *"And in order to see sooner this look which casts a spell on me, I will burn past the restaurants along the highway."*

Above *"The motorcycle stops after a mad run alone, you hear my heart beating for you."*

Right Here is a sepia colored version of the set above, without the young lady. Whereas the above set is identified as Nos. 9190/1 thru 9190/5 this set is identified as No. 9189.

162

Chapter VII: Military

KRIEGSOPFER-WANDKALENDER
der
Nationalsozialistischen
Kriegsopferversorgung

German military postcards are abundant and the two examples on this page show artist drawings of sidecar motorcycles in action. Here the background with it's sunflowers and peaceful cottage nearly gets lost in the dust created as the soldiers pursue their mission.

Bild 40: ⚡-Vorausabteilung in Polen
Gemälde von Schnürpel
Vergrößerungen in Vorbereitung

Idee und Gestaltung: Friedrich Ebert, Berlin W62—9

Wehrmachts-Postkarten Serie 1
Bild 3: Vorgehende motorisierte Infanterie (Kradschützen)

It appears here, that some troops are advancing while others are retreating. This is a great action scene nicely captured by the artist in 1939.

Herr Friedrich Sept. 1939

Mit Genehmigung des Oberkommandos der Wehrmacht

CARTE POSTALE

The caption on this card reads *"Navy soldier driving a sidecar motorcycle."* The back of the card says *"post card"* and gives the publishers name. This is a Japanese card. The image may be a scene in China.

Motorcycling Through History

Heading into WWII this Italian motorcyclist appears to be leading his fellow soldiers into an uncertain future. The motorcycle may be a late 1930s Moto Guzzi.

FOTOCELERE DI A. CAMPASSI-TORINO VIA MAROCHETTI 41— 1941-XIX.   Vera Fotografia   Rip. Interdetta

Here is an amazing portrait of a French soldier posed with his motorcycle squad in the background. What a great image to send home to the family.

CARTE POSTALE

"1914-1915, In Belgium, Belgian motorcyclist on the look out" There is a hand written date on the back of this card that says 18 Sept. 1918. The soldier is standing ahead of his James motorcycle, an early teens model made at Birmingham England. The earliest machines used FN engines. This example may have had a Villiers engine or one of James own design

E. Le Deley, imp.-édit, 127, Boulevard de Sébastopol, Paris.

164

CHAPTER VIII: HUMOROUS

WE HAVE FALLEN OUT!

Motorcycling Through History

CARTE POSTALE
POSTKARTE CARTOLINA POSTALE
POSTCARD BRIEFKAART

What is this gentleman saying as he bids his mother-in-law farewell? From the reaction on her face his gesture is not all that appreciated. This is a turn of the last century card portraying what would be a De Dion tricycle.

M.M. reproduction interdite.

BRIEFKAART. It is apparently not bad enough that this woeful soldier has wrecked his cycle, because that may be the least of his worries. Pleading with the bovine menace is not likely to garner much sympathy and a major goring or head stomping is likely to be inflicted on him.

W. den Boer - Bussum.

CARTE POSTALE
Ce côté est exclusivement réservé à l'adresse

Tricycles were common at the turn of the last century when this card was produced. The card has an undivided back characteristic of cards from that era. The artist is shown as G. Mouton and the small caption reads: "Fv Motocycle" and probably depicts a representation of the De Dion that was first made in France prior to 1900.

Chapter VIII: Humorous

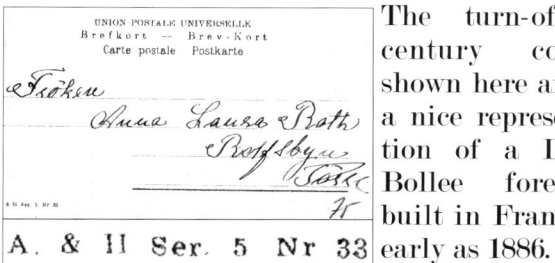

The turn-of-the-century couple shown here are on a nice representation of a Leon-Bollee forecycle built in France as early as 1886.

With this card we are invited to lift the flap and be treated to numerous scenes from Newcastle-on-Tyne. This card was posted in 1914 From Cateshead, England.

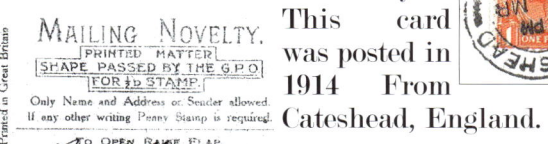

The use of postcards for humorous intent has been going on for over one hundred years as this example from 1901 shows. These overly indulged riders are off to the spa to pay for their sin of gluttony.

167

Motorcycling Through History

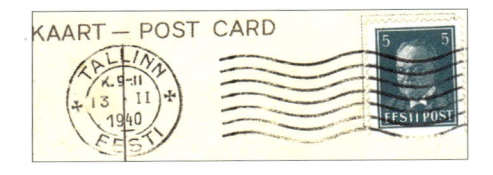

Many a motorcyclist has taken his pooch along with him on his travels. Here the dog's dreams have come true and they are in total command. It is a nice spring scene from Estonia where the winters linger on and the warmth of May brings out the smiles.

This card was printed in Belgium, a country that knows something about motorcycles. They were making cycles at the turn of the last century. Unfortunately, it does not look like they totally have the suspension and handling problems worked out.

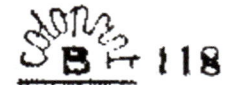

Here see Jack hitting a big ole bump. Look at Jill with her airborne rump. Jack's eyes are wide with awe, but Jill can't believe what she let him saw. Ok! so poetry will never be my true calling.

JACK AND JILL WENT FOR A RUN,
SHE WAS ONLY A SHOWMAN'S DAUGHTER,
BUT THE ROADS ARE BAD AS YOU ALL KNOW,
AND SHE SHOWED WHAT SHE DIDN'T OUGHTER!

Published by BAMFORTH & CO., LTD., Holmfirth, Yorkshire.
"TEMPEST KIDDY" Series.   No. K 83   Printed in England.

168

Chapter VIII: Humorous

This canine couple looks especially well dressed for bikers, but they are from an earlier time. Today's animals riding motorcycles are usually dressed in the blackest of leather, with patches and pins a plenty, and often with an abundance of bare skin hanging out in the wind. Some may be as hairy as this couple but not nearly as cute. Two up, the dog and his bitch are a sight to see.

"Warning of Approach Article IV. (5) He shall give audible and sufficient warning when overtaking foot passengers." This card was posted from Carboldisham England on July 20, 1907. The card is signed on the front and on back says: "Motoritis by Charles Crombie"

From Czechoslovakia comes this lovely card. The date is not legible. Can we assume that this is a lovely young lady motoring through the floral archway? If it is a boy, it will take more than a motorcycle to toughen up his image.

Amag No. 2581

169

Motorcycling Through History

This young fellow, as well as the one to his right and the children on the opposite page were all portrayed by the same artist, shown to be W.F. by the initials. This card was posted and addressed in 1931 to Yugoslavia.

Nr. 1891

Here the handsome young man is about to be disappointed to find that when he arrives at his destination he has lost his letters.

This wonderfully, colorful card comes from the Netherlands and says: *"These two have a grand speed."* The card was printed and published by J. Salmon Ltd. Sevenoaks, England. It bears the following identifying numbers: N-S 12. and 4061. The artist's name is on the front; F.G. Lewin.

170

Chapter VIII: Humorous

This looks like a patient big brother teaching his sister to ride the motorcycle. She appears to be just short of a state of panic. The artist's name in this series of cards is W. Fialiakowski. He was from Austria and lived and worked in Germany.

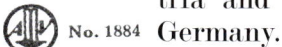

No. 1884

In this picture sister is definitely in a state of panic. Her wide eyed expression says it all. As an older brother to two sisters I can appreciate the fun that this young man is having. This divided back card was posted from Alkmaar In the Netherlands.

Nr. 1883

What a lovely Victorian card this is. It is rich with color and features a group of children out for a ride. This card was posted at Gravenhage, The Netherlands on Nov. 27, 1912.

117

171

Motorcycling Through History

Hand tinting of postcards was not uncommon and examples are shown on this page. Below is an Indian motorcycle from around 1914 although the postcard is newer. This card was a "Fabrication Belge" (Belgium) and was posted in Europe.

The motorcycle here is a Motoconfort which was the name that Motobecane used for it's 308cc single, two stroke machine. It was made between 1925 and 1963. This machine is probably from the 1930s.

This rather gaudy, hand tinted postcard was made in France and interestingly shows an early Indian motorcycle. The card was posted in 1935. In spite of the coloring on this card, the details are exceptionally sharp.

Chapter VIII: Humorous

The card below is Eastern European and a bit later than most cards in this book. It was posted in 1945 and depicts a delivery man using a "ServiCar" style of motorcycle.

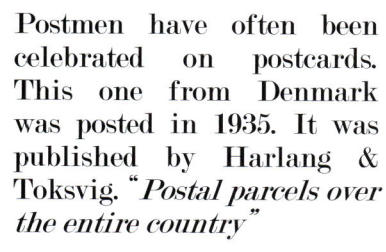

Postmen have often been celebrated on postcards. This one from Denmark was posted in 1935. It was published by Harlang & Toksvig. "*Postal parcels over the entire country*"

The young delivery man at left may be rushing this lovely floral arrangement off to some special friend as a gift. Or he could be carrying a load of apologies for some male indiscretion. This is a divided back card posted on October 9, 1937 from Hungary to Ontario Canada. The only identifying information on the card is a number 4955 found on the back.

173

Motorcycling Through History

To the right is a cute divided back card that was printed in Amsterdam, Holland. The date is unknown, but may be 1917-1918. Like the other cards on this page, this one is an advertisement for the Continental Rubber Company, makers of tires. Do you suppose that the hunter shown here is at all envious of the trapper?

Continental
Caoutchouc- & Gutta-
Percha-Cie., Amsterdam

Postkarte

This German company was founded in 1871 and began producing bicycle tires in 1892, adding automotive tires in 1898. Their products grew to include aircraft applications as well as industrial products. A close association with Daimler-Benz and Porsche led to many successes in car racing.

Continental
Caoutchouc- und Gutta-
Percha-Co., Hannover

Feldpostkarte

This wonderful card is quite dramatic in content and coming during the middle of WWI it has historical significance. The intent is to advertise the Continental Tire Company. The name is quite clearly visible on the front tire. The card shows the date as Dec. 25, 1917.

Continental
Caoutchouc- & Gutta-
Percha-Cie., Amsterdam

174

Chapter VIII: Humorous

Postkarte

The three cards on this page are from the same publisher. They advertise the Excelsior Rubber Works at Hannover-Linden, Germany. The colors and design of this card are especially nice and the scene is peaceful except for the armed soldier.

Hannoversche Gummiwerke, Excelsior A·G.
Hannover-Linden.

The subject matter of these cards appears to be WWI era and the artist name H. Schutz[16] with the number 16 may indicate the date. That would fit with the style of motorcycle depicted. Considering the size of this prisoner, the motorcyclist has his hands full trying to maintain balance. It is a wonder that his front wheel does not come off the ground.

Hannoversche Gummiwerke, Excelsior A·G.
Hannover-Linden.

Postkarte

This soldier appears to be heavily loaded down with the spoils of war. With a pig on his back, chickens and geese in the basket and a couple hundred pounds of bacon in the trailer, breakfasts should be good for some time to come.

Motorcycling Through History

Represented here are the caricature symbols John Bull of England and Marianne of France riding towards victory in the "Great War." Artist: Linsdell, 1917.

Here is a card that was printed in Austria. It has a divided back and was not posted. The identifying publisher mark is: B.K.W.I. 583-3. The image is rather humorous in intent. The privileges of rank are obvious as the young soldier rushes to keep his commander happy.

This is probably a scene from the late teens or early 1920s. The "Great War" is over and people are getting back to a normal way of life. Perhaps this is a French couple riding along the coast feeling the breeze and tasting victory. The only identifying mark from this card is the symbol below.

176

Chapter VIII: Humorous

Here is a little more British humor. The young man seems to have quite a dilemma. I am sure that "Auntie" doesn't want to hear about it. This card was posted in England in 1938 and is shown as "Valentines "Sepiatype" series, Copyright Picture."

The image below is a studio photo taken at Pleasure Beach, Blackpool, England. It was done by Charles Howell, Official Photographer. The card has a simple divided back and has not been used or posted. These two gentlemen present a humorous picture of life at the coast. Assuming they are on holiday, it does not appear as though they will be thirsty.

If this card was meant to be a postcard, it has a completely unprinted back. It is the correct size and weight of an early postcard. The style of the motorcycle appears to be later than most of those in this book, perhaps from the late 1930s. This card should appeal to most traditional motorcyclists. It is quite obvious that the thong bikini is not a new fashion.

177

Motorcycling Through History

Considering that there are now approximately 379 people living in the village of Clarks, this fellow should consider himself lucky that he has found a girlfriend during the time this card was published. There are probably more cows and chickens there than people. Clarks is located in Merrick County, 67 miles from the state capital of Lincoln.

I know a little girl in Clarks, Nebr. that can have a joy ride

Posted in June of 1914, this card was mailed to Bellefonte, Pennsylvania from Pine Glen, PA. A very small number 1674 is printed in the lower left hand corner of the card.

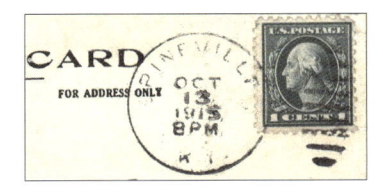

There is no speed limit in Pine Glen

The sentiment expressed here certainly is not unique to Pineville, Kentucky. Serious motorcyclists would certainly avoid any place where their favorite type of ride was not available. Kentucky and other points south of Michigan are riding destinations that draw the serious biker who loves leaning into the corners and testing his nerve and his machine.

Ven yo' ain't got no modorcycle life ain't vorth living in PINEVILLE

178

Chapter VIII: Humorous

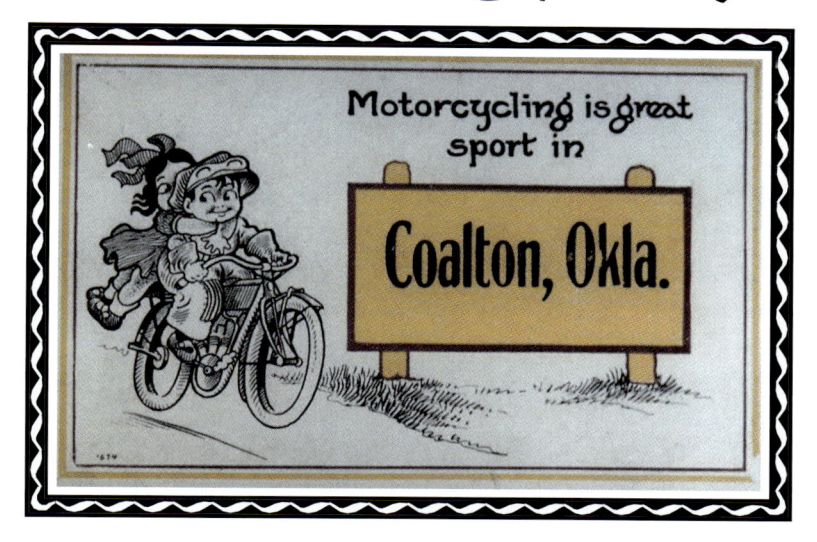

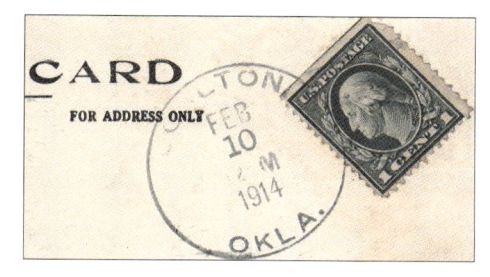

This card bears no identifying publisher marks and is of the divided back design. Posted from Coalton, Okalahoma in 1914 it portrays a happy young couple enjoying the pleasures of the open road, of which Okalahoma has many.

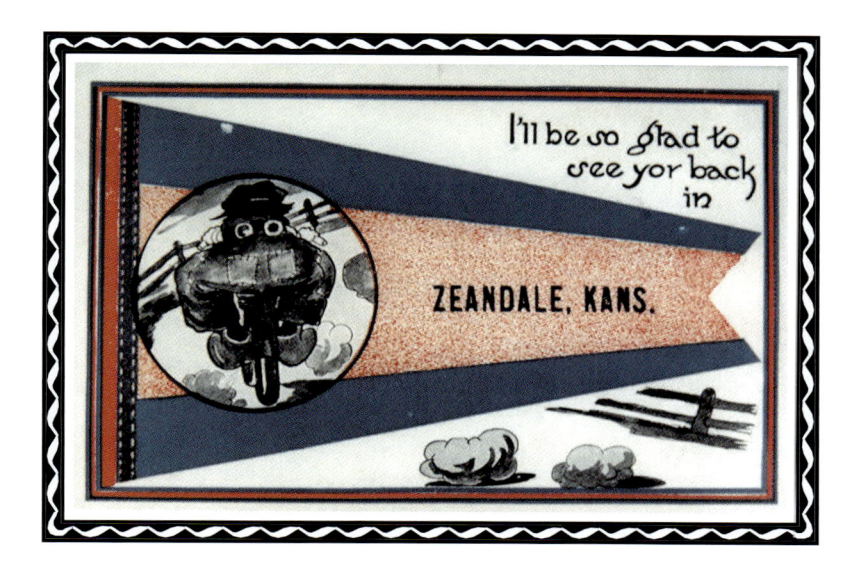

This card, like the one below and those on the next page are all from the same time period, around 1914. Do you suppose that the character in this picture is on his way out of Zeandale? By all appearances he has turned his back on home and is off to some new adventure.

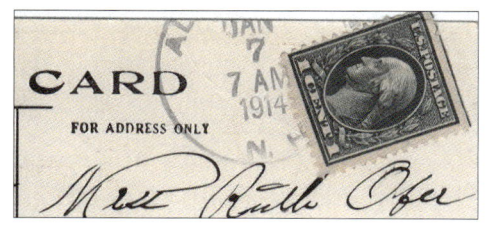

The meaning of this card is not very clear. At first glance it appears that the young lass is driving the motorcycle, but a careful look shows that she is riding side saddle behind her beau. Is she saying to some other suitor, "be careful or I will ride off with someone else".

Motorcycling Through History

This card and the one directly below are obviously from the same publisher, but other than the same identifying number, there are no marks that would indicate where or when these cards were made. This series of cards all seem to date from around 1913-1915.

De girls stichk to me chust like bulldogs, yes

663

The card at right was posted on Dec. 8th from Lima, Iowa, but the year is illegible. What is quite plain is the expression on the face of the motorcyclist. If you have ever owned and maintained your own motorcycle, at some point you should be able to identify with the sentiment expressed here. When this card was published and in the years earlier, motorcycle maintenance was like brushing your teeth, it was a daily endeavor.

I vould like to haf ahold off de guy vot invented modorcycles!

663

Beulah, Michigan is a small town located in one of Michigan's most scenic areas of the N. W. lower peninsula. It is an area that motorcyclists head for, rather than try to get away from. Perhaps because it is such a small town, the lad in this picture is dreaming of a little more excitement.

If I had a modorcycle I bet I vouldn't stick around all de time in Beulah

180

Chapter VIII: Humorous

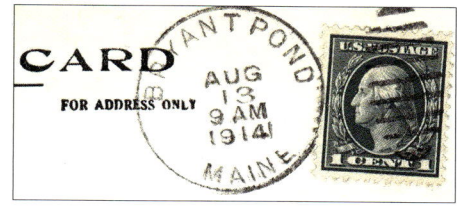

Translated, this card reads *"My life is full of nothing when you are not here in Milton, Maine"*. Said like that, the card does lose some of it's charm. There is no publisher identification on this card, but it is obviously from the same series as the other's shown on adjacent pages.

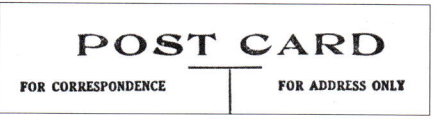

Here is an example of a card similar to those on the previous page. This is a mint, never posted card without any city designation shown in the flag. For the purposes of this example, I have added my home town to the copy. Walled Lake is located in S.E. Michigan, 25 miles North West of Detroit.

It is nice to know that when traveling through the Midwest, a visitor to Columbus will be welcomed with open arms. Ohio, especially southeast Ohio, is a paradise for motorcyclists as the flat land of the north makes way for outstanding curves and hills.

Motorcycling Through History

This card reads: "*I just love feller's with motorcycles*". Hand written beneath this caption is "*But not the motorcycle*". The card was written in 1913 by Lydia and sent to her friend Roscoe in Farmersburg Indiana. It is pretty obvious that she is trying to tell him something.

Translation: "*It is going to cost me a lot of money to get out of Millville*". This card was posted from Michigan to Pinckney, Michigan. It is interesting to note that Millville is a small town in Worcester Co., Massachusetts. One can only speculate as to the crime that this cyclist has committed.

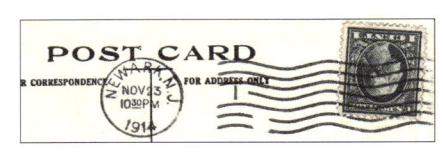

The word is out, no cops in Newark. So get on your cycle and ride. At the very least, it being mid November in Newark there will be a touch of the coming winter in the air. One good fast ride feeling the wind's bite on the cheeks should suffice for an end of season jaunt. Without the law to interfere, this cyclist may get up to 30 MPH.

182

Chapter VIII: Humorous

POST CARD

"I'll stick to you through thick and thin". That's good to know because most of us end up much thicker than thinner. Perhaps wedding vows should read "for better or for worse, for thick or thin".

6508

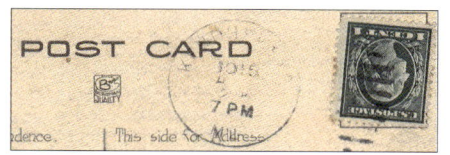

POST CARD

The card shown here is just one in a series featuring these happy Dutch children. Generally, the cards all date from about 1915. This example was posted in 1915 as show by the cancel. These cards were published by the Bergman Co. and copyrighted in 1913.

POST CARD

The Bergman company published a great many postcards and this is another example. Again the theme is Dutch children on the motorcycle. This card has the number 6508 on it's front.

183

Motorcycling Through History

The card shown here and the one below are from the same era. This one was posted from Canada in Feb. of 1915. Dutch children were often used on postcards of this time period and the cards on this page are good examples. In each case the young lady is handling the motorcycle.

There is no publisher shown for this or the others on this page. This one was posted from Hudson, Kansas on Feb. 7, 1916. On this card the "Stafford" referred to is probably the city in Stafford Co. Kansas.

Another from the same series of cards as shown above is this one that is simply a variation of city name. This one was posted from Lake City, Iowa in May of 1915. It too shows the No. 18 on the back of the card.

184

Chapter VIII: Humorous

Shown to the left is card No. 6509. This card depicts a fine young couple enjoying life in Herkimer, New York. The sun is out, the young lady has her man and the motorcycle adds a thrill. Life for them must be about perfect.

Above is another cute card in this series. *"A happy couple in Fort Madison, Iowa"*.

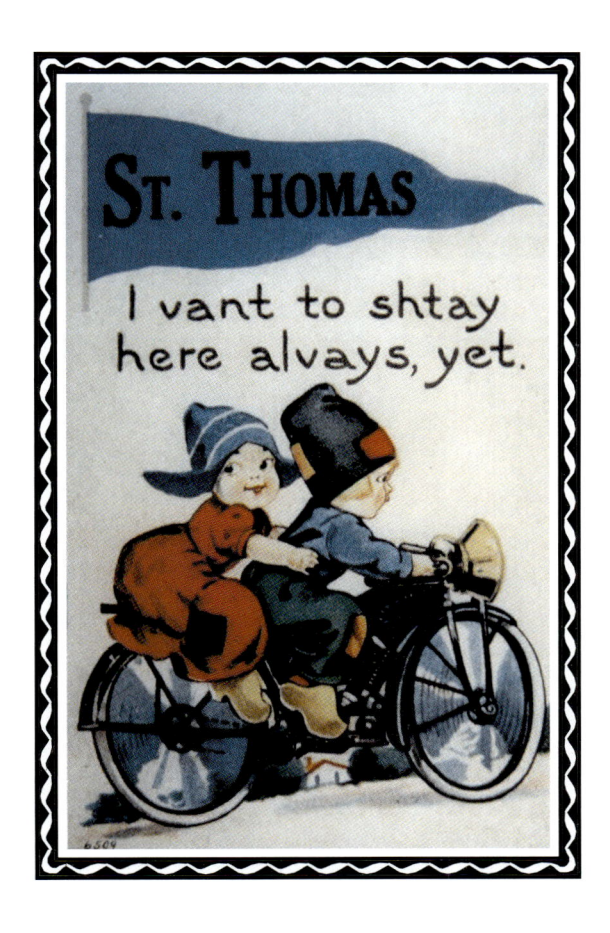

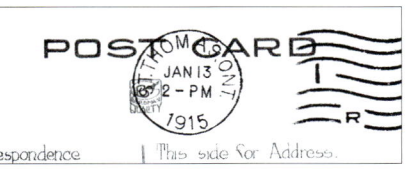

To the left is card 6509 in the series of similar cards shown here. It was posted at St. Thomas Ontario.

185

Motorcycling Through History

The cards on this and the following pages are from a series by the Bergman Publishers. Each carries the number 6508 or 6509 and the copyright symbol of the publisher.
No. 6509

This series of cards were designed so that the pink banner could be printed with the name of a specific community. There could be a great variety of these cards available.
No. 6509

Marshall
Lawd a massy! Dis am some swift town

Youngstown, Ohio.
Lawd a massy! Dis am some swift town

Should one be happy that African Americans are characterized on these cards or offended at the stereotypical nature of the text?

Honey, yo' iss mine sure enough, and I'll hang on

186

Chapter VIII: Humorous

Say, Honey gal won't yu motor froo life wif me?

This card was posted in 1914 from Pennsylvania to Northampton, Mass. It is addressed to a gentleman from his nephew. The message is in a child's hand whereas the address is in a beautifully executed adult hand.
No. 6508

And we'll be as inseparable as the Siamese Twins.

Posted from Gary Indiana in Jan. of 1915 this couple looks as though they are looking for a home on the range. One way or another it appears they will be be together always.
No. 6508

Hoping that your life will be just one big motor joy-ride.

Another in the series of cards by S. Bergman, copyright 1913 is shown here. The postmark is indistinct, but believed to be 1914. It was posted in the U.S. No. 6508 is the identifying number on this card. This cowboy and cowgirl know how wonderful life can be on two wheels.

187

Motorcycling Through History

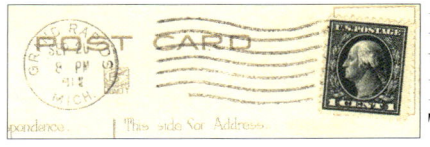

Kids grow up fast in Rochester. This young couple heads down the road with more attention to flirting than watching the traffic.

South Haven, Michigan is located on the shores of Lake Michigan in the S.W. part of the state. The sentiment expressed on this card is pretty accurate for the lovely resort town.

6509

Rochester, N.Y.
This town has 'em all skinned.

So. Haven
Here's the place to whoop it up!

What is interesting about this card is that it is the same basic card as one in the first chapter of this book that is shown under American cycles.

THE GIRLS CAN GO SOME IN
Matson, Mo.
SOME TOWN FOR GIRLS

188

Chapter VIII: Humorous

The S. Bergman Co. of New York published a number of cards with the theme shown here. This particular card was posted on September 19, 1914 from Cloversville, N.Y. Each card bears a copyright mark as shown and the backs are the same.

No. 6508

This young lady is hanging on to her man. A sentiment that says a lot. *"I'm hanging on to the good things in life, believe me."*

No. 6508

"You're good enough to chauffeur me through life"

Cute kids make great subjects for collectors of postcards. Pairing them up with motorcycles has been common over the last 75-100 years.

189

Motorcycling Through History

Although there are a variety of styles of cards from the Bergman series, they fall into two types: 6508 or 6509. It appears that the #6508 refers to the horizontal cards whereas the #6509 cards refer to the vertical cards. The whole series seems to have received copyright in 1913.

No. 6508

I'd like to speed thru life with you, and only you.

This cute card was posted from Essexville, Michigan in 1915. Since these kids feet can't reach the ground, they may be a bit young for motorcycles. 6508

Say, pard, we don't care if we do go the limit.

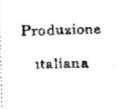

This nice Italian card was drawn by the artist A. Bertiglia. The information along the left edge indicates that the card was produced at Milano and has the date 19-5-917. More so than most, the illustration is quite detailed reflecting well the styling of motorcycles at the time.

190

Chapter VIII: Humorous

"Many Happy Returns" says this card. It was probably posted in 1932 as shown by the postmark and sent from Amsterdam, The Netherlands.

This card and the one below, although nearly identical, are very different. This one is a nicely embossed card that was printed in Germany. It was posted in 1911 to Iowa. The message *"Father, mother and baby off for a picnic"* is different from the card below.

SERIE 7318

Stating *"Pleasant Memories"* this card is a poor imitation of the one above. It is a flat printed card lacking the quality of the other. No publisher identification is provided. It was mailed to Blair Co. PA.

191

Motorcycling Through History

For those who think that having a third wheel is safer, that obviously does not apply to pedestrians. These children are hauling their butts lest they become part of the pavement. This card is from Estonia and was posted in 1927.

W
S+S 9665/3
B

What a stylish rig this is. The flowers are even color coordinated to the paint job of the cycle and sidecar. Posted in 1932 at Rotterdam, this card is quite delightful. *"Many Happy Returns"* reads the caption.

Amag No. 4005

Geese or children, it does not seem to matter to the cyclists on this page, they are all targets. This card is from the Netherlands where the love of motorcycles is frequently portrayed on the postcards from that country. This card is likely from the 1930s.

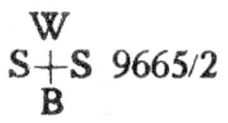

W
S+S 9665/2
B

192

Chapter VIII: Humorous

"*Many Happy Returns*" says the greeting on this card. It is a common sentiment on many of the cards from the Netherlands. This card is probably from very early in the last century and is beautifully embossed and colored. The wicker sidecar sparkles in gold when caught in a reflected light. The colors are brilliant and this Victorian greeting is a delight to view.

HWB SER. 9469

"*Many happy returns*" says this card along with the following poem:

"*A joyful song full
Of beautiful tunes
Look well, this is my wish
in only a few words.*"

This card like the one above sparkles in the light.

Erkal

The postal cancel on this card is especially interesting. Sent from Germany in 1922 this card is brilliant in it's colorful presentation. The gold highlights stand out from the surface and sparkle in the light.

Amag 12230

193

LEVELEZŐ-LAP.

"Czegled in the future"

Czegled is also know as Cegled and is a city in central Hungary, located 42 miles S.E. of Budapest. This card as well as the others on this page all date from around 1913. These fantasy views depict life in the future. Note the early example of hill climbing in the foreground of this image.

Sárik Gyulané, Czegléd.

LEVELEZŐ-LAP.

"Ungvar in the future"

This city also shown to be Uzhgorod, was, prior to WWII a city in S.W. Ukraine a former Hungarian city, N.E. of Budapest. It was taken by the U.S.S.R. in 1946 but is now again part of an independent Hungary.

Levelező-Lap

"Tusnadiirdo in the future"

A reference to this city has not been found, but it is also most likely Hungarian. Admittedly, the motorcycle content in this series of cards is minimal, but I like them.

Dragomán S. J. Székelyudvarhely kiadása

Chapter VIII: Humorous

A great many cards with the theme shown here have been published. They are often amusing and give some insight into how those at the first part of the last century viewed the possibilities for transportation in the future.

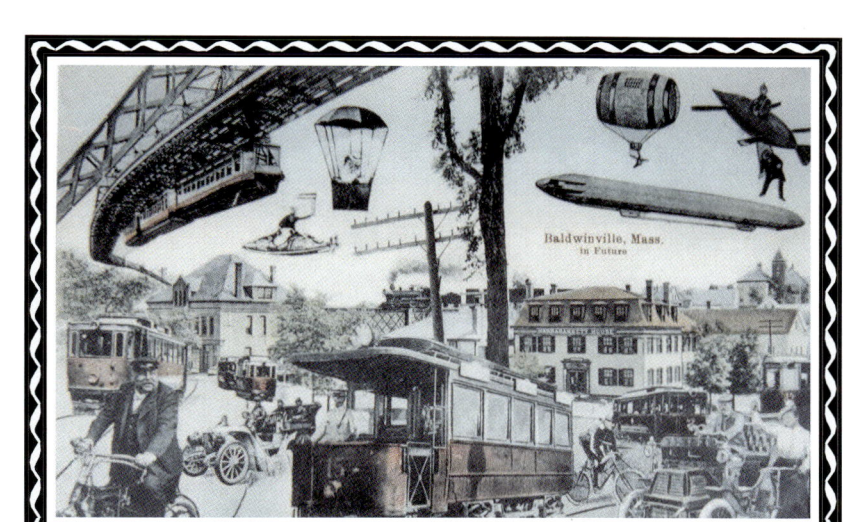

Although this card has very little motorcycle content, the transportation theme is fitting. This is one of my favorite cards which predicts the future as seen from 1908. The card was made in Austria and was published by W.B. Hale, Williamsville, Mass.

These fantasy cards are a lot of fun and give some insight into perceptions about the future at the first part of the last century. From today's vantage point, we can look back and compare the reality of transportation today.

195

Motorcycling Through History

"Groeten van Cor"

This card was posted from the Netherlands in 1930. It is a nice example of the colorful cards that come from that country. Especially nice is the representation of the early BMW motorcycle.

In this image, mom does not seem to be having nearly as much fun as dad. The baby is just bewildered but secure in his basket. *"Out, into the wild"* reads this card. This card is nearly as plain on it's reverse as the card above. The exception is the symbol shown below.

W
S+S 647
B

The card here is another in the Bamforth series which played heavily on humor. As seen in other examples, the motorcycle seems to lend itself to humorous comment. This card was not posted, but gives the following publisher information:. Bamforth & Co. Ltd., publishers. Holmforth (England) and New York. "Witty Comic" series No. 2674 printed in England.

196

Chapter VIII: Humorous

What an idyllic setting for a motorcycle ride. This postcard depicts a scene on the Kenmare Road, Killarney, Ireland. This card may be from the first quarter of the last century. It was printed as a "Valentines" post card of the "Valcolor" series.

In the days of the "horseless carriage" many country folk were probably astounded by the contraptions that came roaring down the lane. This old guy definitely seems bewildered.

"DINGED IF THIS AIN'T THE FIRST TIME I EVER KNEW THEM THINGS HAD COLTS!"

It appears as though this young man is a bit dazed after his encounter with the tree. The crash has been nothing more than a distraction for his lady friend who is intent upon making sure that her face receives it's proper amount of gloss and color. A few cuts and torn clothing do not seem to phase her nor does the spaced out look on her friend.

Nr. 2177

197

Motorcycling Through History

Ladies, Children, and farm animals, beware the crazy cyclist. With one chicken to his toll, the other animals have good reason to scramble for their lives. The "tut tut" from the riders horn is hardly sufficient warning.

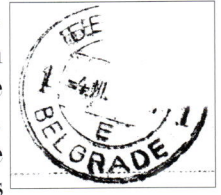

W
S + S 645
B

Lift the flap on this novelty card and see within, scenes from the town of Bury, St. Edmonds, England. This card was mailed from Bury St. Edmonds in Sept. of 1925 and cancelled again in Czechoslovakia on Sept. 10th. The number u 18565 is the only publisher identification found on the card.

This Italian couple and their kitten seem to be having a lovely day as they cruise along with the Mediterranean in the background. Who of us would not enjoy a pleasant ride along Italian country roads?

198

Chapter VIII: Humorous

Like the card next to this one, if a flap is lifted, city scenes are displayed. In this case the town of Rothenburg, located in Bavaria on the Tauber river.

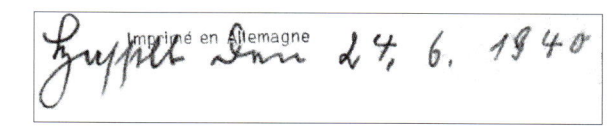

"Good Day from Hasselt". These greetings come from N.E. Belgium. Simply lift the lady's skirt and numerous pleasant scenes from the town of Hasselt fold out for viewing.

These happy children are stirring up a lot of dust, or their engine is burning a lot of oil. One likes to smell the flowers along the way, but dust and oil tend to kill the mood. This card was posted in Belgium in what appears to be 1933.

199

Motorcycling Through History

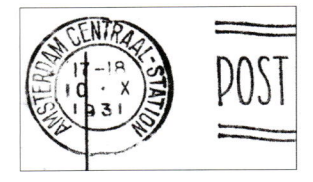

Hikers and motorcyclists never have gotten along well. These issues are as loud today as they were when this image was created. Lets all show respect for each other.

Amag No. 1934

No postmark is available on this card, the stamp having been torn off, but it is undoubtedly from the same time frame as the one above. Those of us who ride motorcycles know how nice a trip to the beach or a secluded spot can be. The couple shown here would certainly seem to agree with that. A bottle of wine and a picnic lunch sounds about perfect.

Amag No. 1929

This card was posted from the Netherlands in 1934 and has a plain, divided back. It does not bear the Amag logo as do the other cards on this page, but it carries the number 1003/4. Most motorcyclists can identify with the peril this couple is experiencing. In this case the young lady is presenting quite a tender target for the canine terrorist.

Chapter VIII: Humorous

PASTKARTE
CARTE POSTALE

The chimney sweep seems to be a popular theme, especially in Eastern Europe. This one and those below are quite similar. The pig was considered a good luck symbol. This card was posted from Latvia in what looks like 1937. The symbols below are found on the card.

Daudz laimes Jaunā gadā!

815

Sveiki sulaukę Naujųjų Metų!

The card at left has a plain divided back and was never posted. Here the little boy and his pig are heading off to do their chimney cleaning chore. The image reminds one of the pop song by Creedence Clearwater Revival with John Fogarty called "Vanz Kant Danz" about a little boy and his pig.

Amag 2801

Viel Glück zum neuen Jahre

It's hard to say if there is any truth to the idea that pigs are a symbol of good luck. For this young man, Mr. Pig seems to have brought a measure of good luck in the form of an attractive young lady. The card says "*Good luck in the new year*". Perhaps the young man will get very lucky.

Amag 2801

Motorcycling Through History

The series of cards on this page are all from the Netherlands. The cozy couple shown here are showing off the advantage of having a sidecar. Of course, this may get you killed, but love makes us do strange things. The dog seems a bit jealous.

Amag 0293

Here is another young couple letting passion get ahead of common sense. These are obviously skilled riders. Don't try this at home folks. The cards on this page each have a simple divided back.

Amag 0293

In this view, we find a much different situation. One supposes that if the young lady forgives him, this young man will have a great deal of making up to do. First the gravel rash on her tush will have to heal. She is not likely to feel like an all over massage very soon.

Amag

202

Chapter VIII: Humorous

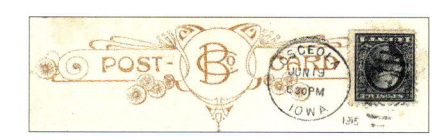

I've got a good spark, so I'm all right.

This fun card was posted from Osceola, Iowa on June 19, 1915. We assume that the young man here is referring to his motorcycle and the condition of it's spark plugs.

HOLMFIRTH BAMFORTH & CO LTD. PUBLISHERS (ENGLAND) AND NEW YORK.

"Never mind how we got here - we're here!"

If this damsel in distress doesn't let go of her man's tie, chances are good that his head is going to explode. Then who will have the last laugh.
"Inter-Art" comique series, Ikay-Geel 7868

A rule of law:

" *A lady must follow her husband. This is not always easy.*"

These may have been words to live by early in the last century, but our ladies today would take affront to the implication that they are followers not equals. Perhaps in France it is different, but in America the spirit of equality is alive and well.

Article du Code:
" *La femme doit suivre son mari.
... Ce n'est pas toujours commode!*"

203

Motorcycling Through History

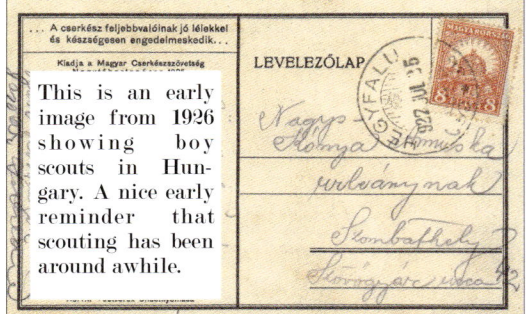

This is an early image from 1926 showing boy scouts in Hungary. A nice early reminder that scouting has been around awhile.

Although there is no information on this card other than the manufacturer's Nr. shown below, it is the same as a known card posted from Germany in 1939. The number on that card was 1233. Three up riding is a great way to see the country as these happy children seem to be doing.

ERIKA Nr. 1270

The early days of motorcycling saw many wicker sidecars attached to two wheelers. It appears that the design shown here never really caught on, but with front and rear handles there could be a practical use beyond carrying passengers. The publishers mark on this card is the same as one on a known card from Estonia. This particular card was obtained from St. Petersbourg, Russia.

NATS. R. TOHVER & K° TALLINN

204

Chapter VIII: Humorous

Published by The Photochrom Co. Ltd. London and Tunbridge Wells, this humorous card was posted to Cambridge England. The card is from the "Exclusive *Celebaue* series, design No. 2323.

Poor Gladys, her dreams of shopping at Harrods are blown in the wind. This is card No. 3268 Published by H.B. Ltd. London, E.C.1.

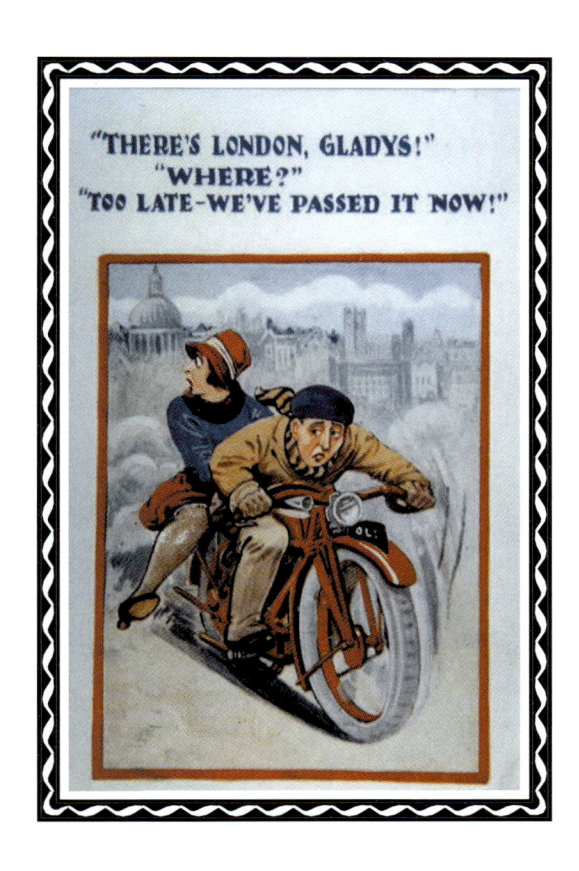

Ok, so the bird lady has gotten her man, but at the cost of his machine. Any true motorcyclist knows his priorities and I suspect that this rider's first priority is flipping over the hill. This card was made in the U.S. and posted to Meshoppen, PA. on November 8, 1939.

205

Motorcycling Through History

The cute couple shown here have found something pleasant to do after their ride into the country. A picnic lunch would make the day perfect. This card was posted on 23 Aug. 1923 from Lewes England. It is from the Regent Series of cards published by The Regent Publishing Co. Ltd. London, N.W.1 and is No 4273.

The Joys of Motoring.

Like the card above, this one is also published by the Regent Publishing Co. Although not posted, it is undoubtedly from the same time period. The message of this card has withstood the passing of time. A pretty smile or a kiss on the cheek and young men lose their direction and stop thinking clearly. What a powerful and wonderful thing love is, if it doesn't get you killed.

Carriage Paid

Here comes the pussy cat patrol. These three felines are leading the way to the next page where cats rule. How can anyone not appreciate a nice warm pussy cat curled up in their lap on a winter day. Unfortunately as motorcycle companions it is more difficult to train them to ride than cuddle..

Zijn vlug genoeg wij wel geweest - Om geluk te wenschen met 't groote feest?

206

Chapter VIII: Humorous

This kitten family seems to have their housing situation well in hand. With a custom built "trike" they are on the road to feline fun. Animals have always provided a good subject for postcard publishers and it was not too much of a stretch to put them on motorcycles. This card was published in Paris by **S.B.W.** and is numbered 505. This card has a simple divided back with an address and message written in French.

Les joies de la famille

Here is another divided back card, but this one was posted. Unfortunately the stamp was torn from the card removing most of the postal cancel with it. This card is numbered 8543 and has the following publishers mark:
    W
S+S 8543
    B

Translated this Dutch postcard reads: *"That is how you drive, but sometimes you need to be a little more careful"*.

Here we have a couple of lovely, Victorian felines out for a ride. Their forecar is ideally suited for a Sunday ride and an afternoon of courting. Forecars were common in the early part of the last century. They were generally made of wicker and often upholstered.

1958

207

Motorcycling Through History

This card was posted in 1915 from Grasmer, New Hampshire. Sidecar driving has always been a tricky business and this couple apparently got a little too close to the fence and now find themselves in a painful position.

Another humorous card in the Bamforth series is No. 1113 shown below from the "Auto comic" series. A popular theme in early humorous cards was losing a spouse or girlfriend from the back of a motorcycle. This card has a nice clean, non posted back and may have been published in the early 1930s.

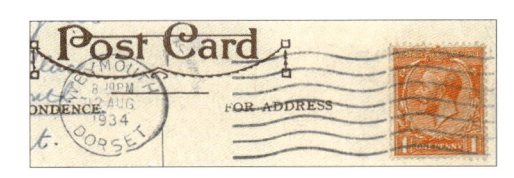

WE HAVE FALLEN OUT!

HOLD TIGHT, MURIEL! I'M TAKING THIS CORNER LIKE I TOOK THE LAST!

Here we see Gladys being left behind, her bloomers in the air. Sport bike riders have to be especially careful about this. The card was published by H.F. Ltd., London E.C.1 and is card No. 4122. It was posted on August 12th of 1934 from Weymouth, Dorset, England to Kingswood, near Bristol.

"HOLD TIGHT, GLADYS—HERE'S ANOTHER SHARP TURN"

208

Chapter VIII: Humorous

This card was posted from Germany to Hartford Connecticut on 25 June 1937. It is a fun image that says *"The newest mobile one family house"*.

N-r. 286

In keeping with the theme on the previous page, here is another tale of woe for the lady. Gert is in a desperate position and the fellow driving the car appears to be keeping a keen eye on her "situation". This card was posted from Blackpool, England on 16 Sept. 1934. It is card No. 4080 in the Bamforth "COMIC" series.

Frogs on motorcycles? Well why not? Many other critters seem to find their way onto cycles. These are Hungarian frogs Ca. 1933 as the postmark indicates. A more handsome pair of amphibians you are unlikely to find.

209

Motorcycling Through History

This postcard is an example of an "hold to light" card. When held that way, the image of a monkey is visible, much like a watermark in the paper. Posted from what is now Croatia, this fun card is a nice example of early postcard humor.

W
S+S 1049
B

It is hard to say what this cyclist is up to, but there is no doubt that getting out of the way is appropriate. The card reads *"The summit is reached"*. If going up hill is a scare, down hill must be an amazing ride. This card was posted at Rotterdam, The Netherlands in 1927.

W
S+S 9677
B

Pogledaj prama svjetlu!

Het toppunt bereikt.

Here are a pair of pups that know how to live. The driver known as "Bonzo" seems to be making eyes at his canine passenger. There is no date cancel on this card, but perhaps the license plate gives an indication of when the card was produced. It says "Ok 42" where 42 could be the year.

"WITH YOU ON THE PILLION, I FEEL LIKE A MILLION!"

210

Chapter VIII: Humorous

This pair of panicked riders better say their prayers since their chance of surviving the peril ahead is slim. The card was posted from Nomme Estonia in July of 1932.

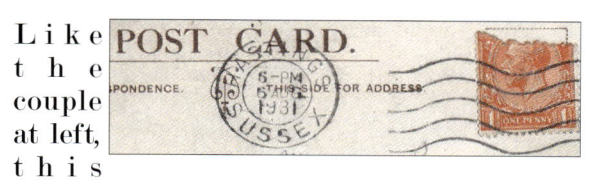

Like the couple at left, this guy better say his prayers. His landing is not going to be pleasant, especially face first. This is card No. A2123 from the XL Series, London, E.C.

"My darling come ride with me". It is hard to say which of these riders is in the worst condition. The lady has definitely landed in an embarrassing position. Her friend has merely shortened his neck. This German card was posted in 1931.

211

Motorcycling Through History

Posted in Budapest, this delightful card portrays the real joy of a peaceful ride in the country. For those of us who ride with a sidecar, the pleasure is as real now as it appears to be for this couple during the first part of the last century.

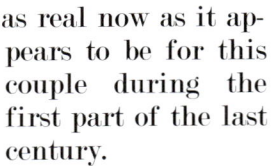

The stamp on this card has been removed and with it the cancellation. Still, it is a lovely card. The young lady seems to have unwrapped a wonderful box of flowers from her beau.

From the examples in this book, there is no doubt that the ladies have a particularly difficult time staying on the back of a motorcycle. It just goes to prove that they should be the ones driving the cycle. This card was posted in Belgium and printed in France.

212

Chapter VIII: Humorous

Many cyclists seem eager to get rid of their women as evidenced by the number of cards that carry that message. This is a "British Throughout, Comic Series" card.

Here is a nice Bamforth card that was posted from Butler PA in 1926. The back of the card says: Kid Comic, printed in U.S.A.

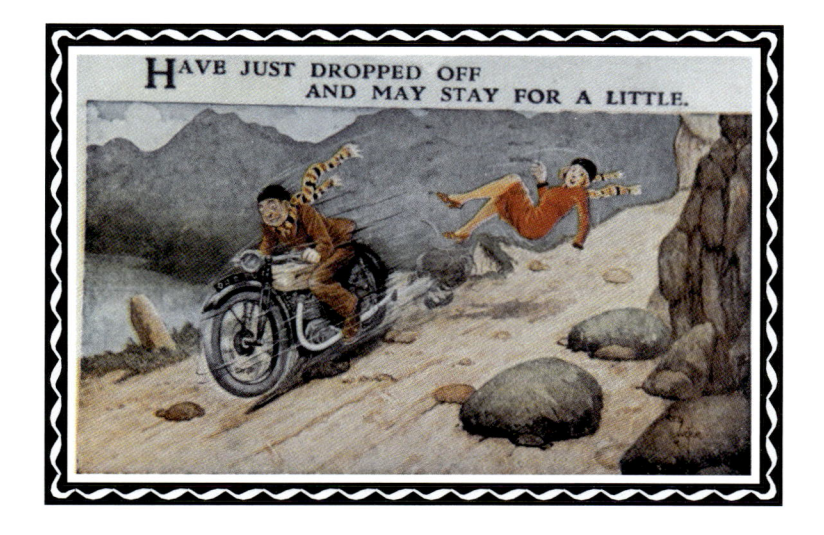

At left, is a card that again was printed in Great Britain. One wonders if the Brits. of the last century ever had tee shirts that read, "if you can read this, my bitch fell off". It's not likely with the British being all proper and such.

213

Motorcycling Through History

Ok, This fellow has a motorcycle, big deal! He obviously has nothing in his head. Would you leave this gorgeous lady behind?

Inter-Art Co., Red Lion Square, London, W.C.
"OUR OWN GIRLS" Series.   No 1022.   *British Manufacture*

The late Victorian era was a time of stylish fashion and graceful designs that retained some of the formality of earlier decades, but bridged the gap between those times and what we think of as more rigid and modern. The elegant couple shown here are dressed wonderfully and have taken to the motorcycle in the spirit of adventure and daring.

"THE GIRL I LEFT BEHIND ME!"

A JOY RIDE

ABC
2258

"Greetings from Herenthals"

This attractive card was posted in Belgium, but the date is unclear. The card was made in France and Herenthals is located in Northern Belgium about 18 miles east of Antwerp.

Chapter VIII: Humorous

Left: A soldier's message to his sweetheart has found it's way onto this card, sent to County Dublin on 7/5/1916. "On active service" is written above the stamp box.

Inter-Art Co., Red Lion Square, London, W.C.
"OUR OWN GIRLS" Series. No. **1021**. *British Manufacture.*

CARTE POSTALE **POSTKARTE** POST CARD
LEVELFZŐ-LAP CARTOLINA POSTALE DOPISNICE BREFKORT
BRIEFKAART KARTA KORESPONDENCYJNA ОТКРЫТОЕ ПИСЬМО.

Printed in Austria.

Above: Although the weather may be frightful, the scene above is just delightful. This Victorian era couple do not seem to care

Fantaisies trichromes. — A. Noyer. — Paris. — *Série nº 12*	
Les Sports galants	48

Left "*Motorcycling, A lovely ride*" is the sentiment expressed on the front of this fantasy card shown to the left. The card is artist signed, Xavier Sagir and was printed in France.

215

Motorcycling Through History

Here is a very colorful boy and girl from Yugoslavia.

What a lovely young couple this is as are the flowers that they carry. It appears as though the artist for this card and the one to the left are the same.

Amag 2905

Amag 2912

Srdačna čestitka imendanu.

Srečno novo leto

This lovely card is quite obviously from the tulip capital of the world. The image is a nice celebration of spring when the tulips are in bloom and young couples are sensing romance in the air or just wind in the face.

W
S + S 8147/III
B

216

Chapter VIII: Humorous

"Greetings from" Rotterdam

Below is another of those cards that has a special fold out pocket that contains photographic images. In this case the views are of the city of Rotterdam. This is a divided back card that was never posted.

This lovely card was printed in France and bears the SERIE No. 3075. The only other information on the reverse of this card is reference to M.D. Paris. "Vive St. Eloi" refers to a village located in N.W. Belgium, West Flanders Province. WWI battles were fought there.

It looks like this old man has a serious problem and it's not his motorcycle. The look on mama's face as she sits in the rain tells it all. This cute card was posted from Antwerp, Belgium in 1925 and is artist drawn by Mauzan.

217

Motorcycling Through History

Coming from Czechoslovakia is this attractive card. It is probably from the 1930s. Wearing their sailor hats, this young couple better keep their eyes on the road. Unfortunately that large floral arrangement must make visibility a bit difficult. They say that love is blind, so perhaps the flowers do not create a serious problem here.

Again we see that love outweighs caution. The young man is going to collect his flowers and letter regardless of the chance for a fall. To his credit, he is well dressed in full riding gear. It appears that this young lady has her eyes on the cyclist and is determined to capture his heart.

The Netherlands seems to have an especially strong passion for flowers as well as motorcycles. So many of the cards that are portrayed in this book reflect that love through the bright colors that flowers provide. This card wishes us *"Many happy returns"*.

218

Chapter VIII: Humorous

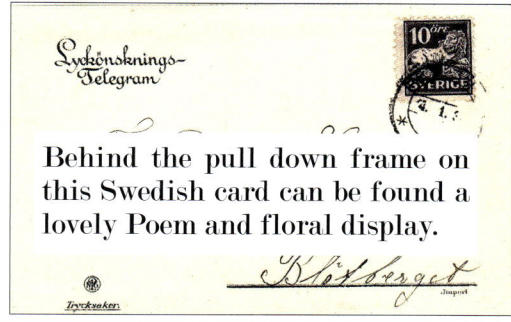

Behind the pull down frame on this Swedish card can be found a lovely Poem and floral display.

"*Many happy returns*"
Is the greeting on this postcard. The cycling couple are heavily weighted down with presents and flowers that must pose a real challenge to carry on the cycle. This card was posted in Amsterdam, but appears to have been printed in Prague.

"*Here you have feather and ink bottle, now write me something*" so the caption reads.

How many of us would take up pen and ink these days to write a letter to someone? Computers, word processors and E-mail have just about killed our writing and penmanship skills. Is that really progress?

W S+S B   7722/2

219

Motorcycling Through History

The card below is a very attractive one from 1933. It was posted from Belgium. The young lady carries a bouquet of what appear to be four leaf clovers. As a symbol of good luck, perhaps they will assure safe riding along life's highways.

Here is a chubby cheeked dandy from the Netherlands. The caption reads "Fearless", but it is easier to imagine this rider as fleeing from the duck. This card was posted in 1919 from Amsterdam.

At right is a card very reminiscent of cards published in later decades by Mainzer. This German card is probably from the 1920s and it's theme of animals riding motorcycles perhaps influenced Mainzer. This is a simple divided back card that states: "Printed in Germany exclusively for Marcel Schumann, importers, 1355 Market St. San Francisco, Calif." This is a fun card with all kinds of things going on.

220

Chapter VIII: Humorous

This unique border surrounds the message side of this card. The greeting on the front of the card says: *"Many Happy Returns."* It was posted from the Netherlands in 1931.

8582 "BEGRO" SERIE ges. gesch.

Hartelijk Gefeliciteerd

The card shown here has a divided back and a simple stamp box that has the number 2252 centered inside. The card was addressed to a person in Amsterdam. Aside from the word "import" printed on the reverse of the card the only other identifying information is the symbol and number shown below. The card reads: *"In Spa (village in Belgium) you don't do things like that".*

HWB   SER 5785

A Spa On'n s'en fait pas

Here is a fun card and one wonders at the significance of the pen and ink bottle. Perhaps if the script were more clear, a translation could be made. In the grass at the lower left of the image are the initials J.L. This card is unused and of simple divided back style. It is probably from the Netherlands and carries the following identifying mark:
W
S + S No. 9839
B

221

Motorcycling Through History

Shown below is a card similar in theme to the one on the previous page. The message seems to be one of, getting a letter on it's way. This plain, divided back card is probably also from the Netherlands.

W
S + S   9874/2
B

Posted from Nurnberg on July 28, 1939, this card presents a cute image of a boy and girl having a flat tire dilemma. The card reads, *"The best wishes for your birthday"*.

Nr. 1233

Unlike so many cards that show a husband or boyfriend, dumping his lady, here is a bit of a switch with this dashing cyclist leaving his buddy in the dust. This card was copyrighted in 1912 by J.J. Marks, New York. It is the "comics" series number 26.

222

Chapter VIII: Humorous

Posted in 1935 and celebrating the Silver Jubilee is this card. It is Camp Silhouette Series No. 21 published by The Photochrome Co. Ltd. London and Tunbridge Wells. This card and the one below are somewhat unusual in their style.

Although this card is by the same publisher as the one above, the back design has changed. It is Camp Silhouette Series No. 10. The card is not dated, but may be earlier than the one above, perhaps WWI. The back says: *"We are still in the mud up to our asses. We set off yesterday and were turned back by a dispatch motor as they were made up with troops at Southampton. We are going tomorrow the 29th for France. Love to all, Harry."*

For those of us who are cat lovers, the image here is not a pleasant one. This poor kitty has probably used up all of it's lives as this French Gendarme races to his next assignment. The caption reads "position". This cat's position is obviously very precarious. This card is a bit unusual in it's line art format not often seen featuring motorcycles.

223

Motorcycling Through History

Motorcycling will always have it's critics. Sometimes the biggest critics are the most ignorant. This is card No. 4260 published by H. B. Ltd., London, E.C.1. Entire British Promotions.

This is another fun Bamforth card. It has not been used and is from the series "Automobile Comic." It is No. 449 printed in the U.S.A. Although sidecars are considered family transportation, this is getting a little carried away. On the plus side, hard right turns should not pose a problem of the chair coming up.

As in the image above, this one seems to be pushing the limit of safe family transportation. Someone should tell this couple what is causing their seating problem. Ride more, play less. This card from the "Domestic Comic" series is No. 7018, Bamforth Comic, Printed in U.S.A.

Chapter VIII: Humorous

This is card No. 2688 from the "witty Comic" series printed by Bamforth & Co. Ltd, Holmfirth, England and New York, printed in England. It carries a one penny stamp and was posted in July of 1930 from Skeoness Lincs., England A common theme in many early humorous cards seems to draw attention to the female anatomy as depicted in the cards on this page.

Shown here is another Bamforth and Co. Ltd. Card. This is No. 305 in the "Art Comic" series and was printed in the U.S.A. This and similar captions can be found on quite a few humorous cards from this era.

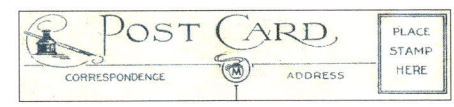

Compared to the behinds shown in the above cards, this card at least attempts to shown a pleasant contrast. What's with the old fellow and the young thing? Oh! right, that's me driving and only a youthful dream riding behind me. This is card series No. 481 General Comics 24 Designs. The card was made in the U.S.A.

225

Motorcycling Through History

What can be said about this image? The racial overtones are obvious. This card was addressed but never posted. It has a divided back and was to be sent to an address shown as "Kopingebra" probably in Sweden.

It's not clear what this rather unkempt gentleman is saying. Perhaps he is referring to the relatively low cost of motorcycle transportation. This card was posted to Cambridge IL.

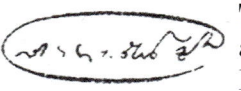

The date is not clear, but an identical card was know to be posted in 1908.

Keeping with the theme of those cards on the previous page is this offering, published by the M. Kashover Co., Los Angeles, California. One suspects that the load limit of this motorcycle has been grossly exceeded.

Chapter VIII: Humorous

The cards on this page are all from the Bamforth publishers. This one is from their comic series, No. 1939 and was printed at Holmfirth, Yorkshire, England. This card has not been posted, but seems to be a bit more modern than the others on this page.

This card Is No. 301 and says: "Imprime En Angleterre." This couple somehow does not seem to fit anyone's image of what cyclists should look like, regardless of the era from when they are portrayed. He is no James Dean.

From the "Vacation Comics" series is this Bamforth card which was printed at Mohegan Lake N.Y.. It is shown to be card No. 13518. A one penny U.S. Washington stamp is affixed to this card and it was posted on July 24th 1935 at Franklinville, N.Y. The gentle innuendo of this message slaps you right in the face.

Motorcycling Through History

Risqué French postcards are famous, but not too many are found with a motorcycle. Compared to modern motorcycle pin-ups this young lady is far too overdressed. When these photo's were taken the poses were especially daring even to the point that the publisher did not seem to want to be identified, if the symbol at left is any indication.

The motorcycle shown here is an Ravat. It was produced in France, possibly from as early as 1898 until the late 1950s. It's styling seems consistent with features from the late teens of the last century. The company, like many other motorcycle manufacturers started out as a bicycle factory. It used a number of engines from other manufacturers in it's frames.

I'M PICKING UP WELL HERE.

The Regent Publishing Co. Ltd.
London N.W. No. 4426

If all it takes is a neat cap, low slung handlebars and a bright red paint job, those of us without then better re-evaluate our mode of transport. Either that or quit trying to be young.

228

Chapter VII: Humorous

"On a bench in Konigsbrunn moans Mirzl: "this hole is my undoing".

This card and the one below definitely go beyond risqué and show that at the turn of the last century pornography was available, but with a sense of humor. Laid out on a bench that reads "beautification" this passionate couple are doing their best to enjoy the beauty of nature.

Palos 707

"Voata! come look at the two city slickers; he bites the belly and can't find the hole".

This officer better go back to basic training and learn something about navigation and orienteering. It is obvious to the observer behind the fence that the soldier is way off course. This lustful couple may be better off using the sidecar as a means of finding their way.

Palos 707

"Ok, enough of this biggest swindle, it is high time".

There is no doubt that this cyclist is fleeing from the result of his careless ways. Some would condemn this sorry soul, while others would merely chastise him for being stupid and getting caught. Let this be a warning to those with too much testosterone and no sense. You play, you going to pay.

S+S W/B 1452

229

Motorcycling Through History

As on the previous pages, this postcard continues the risqué theme with some mild innuendo. Poor George doesn't seem to have a clue about motorcycles or women. Although this card was never posted, it is safe to place it from the 1930s. Poor George. You could hit him with a hammer and he would still be dumb as a stump.

Here is a cute card from the Netherlands. The young lady is out for a thrill but worries about what her parents may think. Translated the card reads: *"Drive, drive, as fast as you can, but what will mom and dad say?"*. Other than a dividing line and four lines for an address, there is nothing else on the reverse of this card.

This card was printed in Great Britain. It states "Valentines Series" on the back. It has a divided back, but no other helpful information. The cyclist shown looks as though he has been in the saddle much too long as he slumps from fatigue. He is either carrying a large lunch on his back or he has a particularly nasty growth back there. If he is *"on pleasure bent"* the lunch theory probably holds more merit.

230

Chapter VIII: Humorous

This card and the other three from the same set are especially colorful and nicely detailed.
B. K. W. I. 632-1

At one time or another, most motorcyclists have encountered the concern expressed on the face of this rider.
B. K. W. I. 632-2

This divided back card was posted from Budapest, Hungary, probably around the mid 1930s. It appears as though a pretty formal luncheon is under way and perhaps a little flirting. The young lady, powdering her nose seems intent on winning this young man's heart. His motorcycle is definitely set up for two and ready to carry them along life's highway.

Amag 0433

Motorcycling Through History

If dad is trying to look like he knows what he is doing, I as well as the kids are a bit skeptical. B. K. W. I. 632-3

An enjoyable outing with the family dog. What a great way to travel.
B. K. W. I. 632-4

This early color card gives an idea of what roads were like for early cyclists. In this case the roads are in Italy. This is a great period scene where the cycle is only incidental. The photo is probably from 1916 as shown below.

Chapter VIII: Humorous

Shown on this page and the next are a series of cards that are believed to have been printed around 1910. None have been posted and there is little to identify them. They are all artist signed by the same individual and each bears it's own series number. On this card is an image of sidecar racing, still popular today although today's sidecar racers show little resemblance to the one shown here. One thing that has stayed the same is the passenger, known as the "monkey". B.K.W.I. 384-1

O, welche frohe Lust!

The coloring and humorous intent of these cards makes them extremely desirable. On this card we see a couple off on a picnic. The rotund lady passenger seems to be carrying a feast of goodies that when spread out on the blanket should provide an afternoon of culinary delights. One suspects that the lady shown here is a picnic professional.

B.K.W.I. 384-2

Here the strong arm of the law seems to be showing no mercy to the cyclists who have obviously brought to an end the life of one fatted goose. No matter how the cyclist pleads his case or the lady laments the sad incident, a fine is about to be imposed. If there is any justice at all, at least the couple should get to keep the goose.

B.K.W.I. 384-3

233

Motorcycling Through History

This smug looking dog does not realize how close he has come to looking like the goose in the previous card It is obvious that the cyclist is doing his best to prevent a collision at the expense of his shoe leather and nerves. With the handlebars cranked at such an angle it is likely that a little shoe leather will be the least of his worries. He is going down. One suspects that the grinning pooch will soon have that smile wiped off his face.
B.K.W.I. 384-4

Now, this is a grim scene. An obvious collision has resulted in a badly damaged front wheel. If the lady is putting her faith in her partner to fix the machine, she will be old and gray waiting for it to happen. One cannot even guess what he is doing with a set of wood chisels. The crescent wrench and air pump yes, but chisels no. And what is the lady thinking or doing with a tin of what appears to be oil. This whole scene is bizarre.
B.K.W.I. 384-5

When one thinks about sidecarring, this is a scene that often comes to mind. What better than to take the whole family out for a spin in the country or to a picnic as this family seems destined. No doubt that the family dog will be glad to see them arrive at their destination. Frankly, this is just too much family togetherness. Father does appear to look a little grim, an expression worn by most of us who have traveled with children. B.K.W.I. 384-6

Chapter VIII: Humorous

The color here is unusual, but not for the artist who is represented. Yves Diey was born in France and was a member of the Salon des Artistes Francais. He is famous for his paintings of nudes. Born in 1892, he lived until 1984.

*Impr. A.D.I.A. - 55, ch. de St-Roch — NICE —
SERIE 20 — N° 23 — La Course au Bonheur*

It is pretty certain that this lout has not won a friend with his stupid antics. A gentleman would stop the cycle, get off and then make a proper ass out of himself.

*HOLMFIRTH
BAMFORTH & CO., LTD., PUBLISHERS (ENGLAND) AND NEW YORK, SERIES NO. 2011
PRINTED IN ENGLAND.*

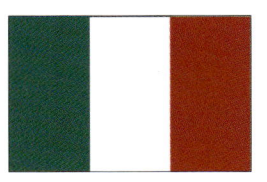

"I've spotted a nice girl."

Proudly flying the Italian flag, this rider looks as though he owns the road. The dog has no illusions about that as he hauls his butt out of harms way.

Vistato dall' Ufficio Revisione Stampa di Milano · N. 1972

235

Motorcycling Through History

This card has a hand written message dated 1922, but it was not posted. How do the fat, old rich guys, get all of the pretty young ladies? It definitely is not just an Italian thing. The young man on the bicycle is going to have to pedal pretty fast to win this race.

2806 - 2

La moglie deve seguire il marito!!

I sure would like to know what this card says. If anyone out there knows, I would appreciate the information. It is apparently an Arabic dialect and inquiries I have made to Algeria have not come back with an answer. So folks, make up your own caption and have some fun.

Agence du *Petit Parisien*, Alger.

Cliché LOBRY. Alger. — Impr. Algérienne

Matenant j'en i bian gagni l'arjan dis of et dis poles ji proumine challa vic mon famille.

This unique card has a frontal, fold out pocket that contains ten individual snapshots of the town of Paignton. The card was printed in Great Britain and has a one penny stamp. The date is not legible.

PRINTED PAPER
MAILING NOVELTY
SHAPE PASSED BY THE G.P.O.
FOR PRINTED PAPER POSTAGE RATE
Only Name and Address of Sender Allowed
If any other writing, Letter Postage is required
TO OPEN RAISE FLAP

A HAPPY COMBINATION AT PAIGNTON

236

Chapter VIII: Humorous

Coolangatta is located on the border of Queensland and New South Wales, Australia. It is at the southern end of Queensland's Gold Coast. A unique pocket on this card opens to reveal pictures of the town. The card was printed in Great Britain and is No. 1419 in the Valentine's series.

"Greetings from the resort, Berneck. Recently arrived in a high mood". It looks like this couple's mood is about to change. Perhaps the resort that they are visiting has a hot mineral bath so they can soak their bruised and battered bodies.

Nr. 288

1931

How long has it been since you have seen one of these flying about? This is marvelous German inventiveness. A sausage casing for the balloon, a boat for the water and a motorcycle for the street. *"You sometimes want a better flavour so simply fly into the air."*

Nr. 288

237

Motorcycling Through History

These two rigs appear to be ridden by members of the "American Sidecar Association". Although their helmets are a little strange, their expressive faces tell us about the joy and pain of this type of three wheel adventure. Sidecarists are full of fun and it is not unusual to find them creating a little mayhem for the sole purpose of a good laugh, except the couple in the front rig do not seem to be laughing. What's their problem?

Beinah' hätten wir's vergessen zum Geburtstag zu gratulieren.

Here is a fanciful creation that is a combination Servicar and front wheel driven machine similar in design to the German and Czech designs found in real photo cards earlier in this book. For both the driver and the passenger, not to mention the pooch, this appears to be a pretty elegant means of transportation.

W
S+S 4444
B

Lift the sidecar wheel and you will find hidden beneath, a series of photo's of Luxembourg, Belgium. This type of card was quite popular as a means of providing a souvenir of ones visit to a another city. There are a number of examples shown within the pages of this book. This particular example was not posted and was probably kept as a true souvenir of the purchasers travels.

Souvenir de Luxembourg

238

Chapter VIII: Humorous

The card at left and the others on this page are a unique set all acquired at different times and places but with the same individuals in different poses. Each has a cute caption written on the front. This one says: *"I tried to fix the sparking-plug to the tune of "Whistling Rufus"."*

Above, a handsome couple state that *"this is what we do when the motor goes wrong".* It is probably a Ca. 1910 Premier built at Coventry, England. These cycles had large V-twin engines with outside flywheels. Each of these three cards was printed by Davidson Bros., London & New York. Printed in London.

There is no telling how many cards there are in this series, but at least the one at left was posted giving a clear date of 1910. It was posted in England to an address in Sussex.

239

Motorcycling Through History

Here is yet another card in this humorous series. A short note on the back of this one says *"From yours, on the other side"*. It appears as though the card was posted at Kincardineshire, Scotland and is probably from 1910 as in the one on the previous page.

DAVIDSON BROS., LONDON & NEW YORK. PRINTED IN ENGLAND.

So near and yet so far, from Home, Sweet Home!

These well dressed motorcyclists seem content to push their transportation, saying *"It's a pleasure to have a break down"*. The headlight on this cycle is lit using gas generated in the vertical cylinder behind the handle bars. The two-part generator tank mixed water with calcium carbide which chemically reacted to produce acetylene gas. With a high power loupe, it is possible to read *"protected T R"* on the engine case of this cycle.

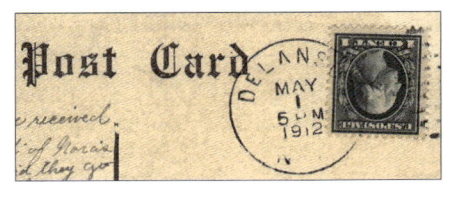

It's a pleasure to have a break down!

If there is a hidden meaning in the message on this card one has but his imagination to rely on for some answer. A cycle for two, parked on a quiet country road and no one in sight could mean that it is spring time and love is in the air. Or it could mean that the damn thing is just broken.

Something wrong somewhere!

240

Chapter VIII: Humorous

Posted in 1932 from Margate, Kent, England, this card shows a chubby cheeked cyclist and his passenger. She intent on applying her makeup. She is different from today's women only in that today makeup is applied while driving and looking in the rear view mirror. Published by Valentines "Merritt" Postcards, Valentine & Sons Ltd. Dundee and London. No. 2213

This team of riders seem an unlikely pair. The driver with his nose red as a beet and his butt big as a boat is protecting his friend from the wind and cold. The passenger seems a bit unnerved and hangs on tightly to his friend. Two-up riding is great fun when cold and fear are not along for the ride.

Here is a lovely springtime scene with the young lady taking her best friend for a ride. Her friend has eyes for the suitor trotting along beside them.

241

Motorcycling Through History

Should these pathetic looking soldiers ever see an actual enemy, they may be in real trouble. Their look at encountering a playful dog and tormented chickens makes one wonder how they would handle a situation where automatic weapons are pointed at them. This is an artist drawn card with the signature of the artist shown below.

57 Verlag Hunziker, Militar-Badarf, Aarau

By The look on her face, this lovely cyclist appears to be taking great pleasure in seeing her friend land on his goat. Perhaps she is taking revenge for all the unhappy ladies seen in this book who have found themselves in the position that this fellow is headed for. She must be a very experienced cyclist to have kept from going over the handle bars. *"Don't scare the goat".*

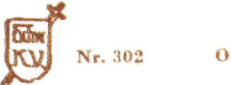

Do you think that this policeman is laughing at the cyclist and his young friend who are pushing their cycle? It is no laughing matter for those of us who have found ourselves in the same position. If you want to get your heart pumping, this is a good way to do it. Add the weight of a sidecar and you will quickly wonder why you have not spent more time on a treadmill or doing other cardio vascular workouts that would prepare you for a breakdown situation.

242

Chapter VIII: Humorous

Will be detained tonight. Official business.

The Cycle and Automobile Trade Journal is the leading and largest motoring publication in the world. Each issue contains the largest number of reading and advertising pages. The news is accurate, interesting and valuable and its advertising pages are a guide for well-informed buyers. It is published by the CHILTON PRINTING COMPANY
Market and 49th Streets   Philadelphia, Penna.

As indicated in the text above, this card was published by the Chilton Printing Co. Every mechanic knows Chilton for it's books on automotive repair.

Wir gratulieren herzlichst zum Geburtstag.

These riders appear to be late for someone's birthday party. They are obviously rushing somewhere as they send out birthday congratulations. At the very least, they are late for the holiday chapter of this book. Such a nice card does not deserve to be left out and this family can reside at the end of this book singing better late than never.

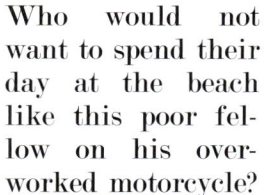

W
S + S   444
B

Avide d'air et d'espace.
Een reisje aan de zee gaat noch al mee.
I take every day a lot of fresh air.

Who would not want to spend their day at the beach like this poor fellow on his overworked motorcycle? Perhaps in Belgium, getting fresh air has a whole different meaning. I guess there is very little likelihood that this cyclist is going to get a sunburn. Although difficult to read, it looks like this card was posted in 1937.

Rokat   191

243

Motorcycling Through History

Coming from the Netherlands is this delightful greeting. It reads: "Lots of luck in the new year". The reverse has a long hand written message, but does not bear a stamp or date. The card is a divided back style. The children riding the sidecar rig seem oblivious of the cold. At least with three wheels they are less likely to fall over. 	EAS 1745

CARTE POSTALE
La Correspondance au recto n'est pas acceptée par tous les pays étrangers
(Se renseigner à la poste)

Correspondance | Adresse

Sidecar lovers will appreciate this great card. It appears hand drawn and hand colored by the artist who signed and dated it in 1914.

What a fantastic card this is. It's depiction of automobile and motorcycle racing from the turn of the last century is brilliantly captured by the artist. The card is French and although undated is very early. This is a particularly rare card. The message at the top of the card reads: *"Cruel engine!!! On top of which of these machines my elegance catches your attention."*

244

Chapter VIII: Humorous

Here is a lovely German birthday greeting sent in 1931 from Chemnitz, Germany.

Ok, where is the motorcycle, you ask. Use your imagination friends, Santa has obviously left it parked so that he can deliver presents house to house on foot. Either that or it's deadline time to get this book to the printer and I'm short one picture. If you are really lucky, Santa may bring you one of these books next Christmas.

And finally, for my fishing friends, here is a little something for you. Even though you would rather have some smelly fish hanging on your line than be saddled up with your legs around some two wheeled dream machine, so be it. I will think of you as I feel the wind in my face, the freedom of the open road and the adventures ahead. I will know that you are bobbing in a boat, going no where with the sun baking your brains and if I feel like it, I'll pick up a salmon at the market, a sure thing.

© 1912, by R.S. Johnson Jr. Wampum, Wisconsin.

245

APPENDIX : POSTCARD RESOURCES

International Federation of Postcard Dealers, IFPD Inc. P.O. Box 1765 Manassas VA 20108. *"Although primarily a dealers organization, the I.F.P.D. protects the interests of both collectors and dealers. Its purpose is to encourage professionalism, increase confidence, strengthen ethics as well as advance and promote the postcard hobby worldwide".* This organization maintains a list of all member dealers.

Postcard Collector, P.O. Box 1050, Dubuque, Iowa, 52004
Monthly publication on all aspects of postcard collecting
www.postcardcollector.com

Barr's Postcard News, P.O. Box 601, Vinton, Iowa, 52349
Semi monthly publication on all aspects of postcard collecting
E-mail: BarrsPCN@aol.com

Playle's Postcards,
On-line postcard auctions
www.playle.com

E-Bay, on the World Wide Web
www.ebay.com

On E-Bay, the following sellers have always given me excellent service: "Globalhistory", "Archcity", "Rustam73", "jabuka2001", "A-vue", "sandymillins", "Vucic", "cards.de", "varispc", and "postcarduniverse".

Card-Guard, 39 Monmouth St. Dept. PCD, Red Bank, NJ 07701
Supplies for collectors
www.monmouthstampandcoin.com

Bags Unlimited, 7 Canal St. Rochester, NY 14608
Postcard supply center
www.bagsunlimited.com

For anyone interested in starting a postcard collection, the best place to begin would be by contacting "The Postcard Collector" or "Barr's Postcard News" for a subscription to their periodical. In addition, your local library and book store will have reference material that can be of interest. Lastly, do not forget to investigate local postcard clubs for guidance and friendship.

BIBLIOGRAPHY:

The books listed below were referenced in the preparation of this title.

Bacon, Roy; British Motorcycles of the 30's, Osprey Publishing, 1986

Bacon, Roy; The Illustrated Motorcycle Legends, Norton, Chartwell Books, 1996

Bacon, Roy; The Illustrated Motorcycle Legends, BSA, Chartwell Books, 1995

Bacon, Roy; The Illustrated Motorcycle Legends, Triumph, Sunburst Books, 1993

Brazendale, Geoff; The Sidecar a History, self published, 1999

Bull, Maureen A.; New Zealand's Motorcycle Heritage, 1899-1931, Masterton Publishing House, 1981

Camp, Robert Gordon; The Illustrated History of Sunbeam, Haynes Pub. 1989

Clymer, Floyd; A Treasury of Motor Cycles of the World, Bonanza Books,

Clymer, Floyd; Historical Motor Scrapbook, Vol. 1-6 1944-1950

Clymer, Floyd; Historical Scrapbook, Foreign Motorcycle edition, 1955

Collins, Paul; British Motorcycles since 1900, Ian Allan Publishing, 1998

Columbia House / New York, Orbis Publishing Ltd., London, 1977. The World Of Motorcycles, An Illustrated Encyclopedia, 22 volumes.

Girdler, Allan; The Harley-Davidson and Indian Wars, Motorbooks Int. 1997

Hatfield, Jerry & Halberstadt, Hans; Indian Motorcycles, Motorbooks Int. 1996

Hatfield, Jerry; Inside Harley-Davidson, Motorbooks Int. 1990

Hinreichsen, Horst; Motorcycles of the Wehrmacht, Schiffer Publishing Ltd. 1994

Holliday, Bob; Motorcycle Panorama, Arco Pub. Co. Inc., 1975

Hough, Richard; A History of the Worlds Motorcycles, Harper & Row, 1977

Louis, Harry & Currie, Bob; The Classic Motorcycles, 1896-1950, E.P. Dutton & Co. Inc. 1976

BIBLIOGRAPHY:

Mitchel, Doug; Harley-Davidson Chronicle, Publications Int. Ltd. 1996

Orchard, C.J. & Madden, S.J.; British Forces Motorcycles 1925-45, Sutton, 1997

Page, Victor W.; Motorcycles and Sidecars, Norman W. Henley Pub. 1921

Partridge, Michael; Motorcycle Pioneers, David P. Charles Publisher, 1976

Paulson, Tim & Winkowski, Fredric; Harleys, Popes, And Indian Chiefs, Wellfleet Press, 2001

Porazik, Juraj; Motorcycles 1885-1940, Galley Press, 1983

Rafferty, Tod; The Complete Illustrated Encyclopedia of American Motorcycles, Quadrillion Publishing, 1999

Reynolds, Jim; Best of British Bikes, Patrick Stephens Ltd. 1990

Sheldon, James; Veteran & Vintage Motorcycles, B.T. Batsford Ltd. 1961

Sucher, Harry V.; Inside American Motorcycling, Infosport, 1995

The Antique Motorcycle Club of America magazine on CD Rom, 1954-1995

Tragatsch, Erwin; The Illustrated Encyclopedia of Motorcycles, Hamlyn, 1977

Walford, Eric W. M.I.A.E.; Early Days in the British Motor Cycle Industry, The British Cycle & Motor Cycle Manufacturers And Trade Union Ltd. 1931

Ward, Ian & Caddell, Laurie; Great British Bikes, Little, Brown & Co. 1994

Wilson, A.J.; Motorcycles And How To Manage Them, Iliffe & Sons Ltd., 1902

Wilson, Hugo; The Encyclopedia of the Motorcycle, Dorling Kindersley, 1995

Wise, David Burgess; Historic Motor Cycles, Hamlyn Pub. Group Ltd., 1973

Youngblood, Ed; A Century of Indian, MBI Publishing, 2001

INDEX:

A.J.S (England) 106
Adler (Germany) 64
American Motor Co. 102, 103
Ariel (England) 68, 92
Aurora Machinery Co. 33, 34
Automobile Trade Journal 103
B.M.W. (Germany) 64, 93, 142
B.S.A. (England) 50, 52, 59, 106, 156, 158
Baker, F.E. 108
Bartha, GY 95
Beardmore-Precision (England) 108
Beardmore, William 108
Betman, Siegfried 142
Birthday greetings 136, 137, 138, 243, 245
Bonzo, 126, 210
Boy scouts. 204
Brookings Co. Fair 37
Butterfield, Arthur Hughes 50
Butterfield, William 50
Campion (England) 140
Champoiseau, Rene 78
Chimney sweep, 111, 201
Christmas Holiday, 126, 127, 128, 129, 130, 131, 132, 133, 134, 245
Chubbuck, S.J. 82
Cissac, 77
Clark, R.L. 38
Cleveland (CT and Ohio U.S.A.) 39
Clyno (England) 54
Columbia Bicycles 32
Consolidated Mfg. see Yale 31, 106
Continental Pneumatic 72, 74, 174
Coogan, Richard B. 23
Curtiss (New York, U.S.A.) 31, 36, 39
Curtiss, Glenn H. 36, 39, 104
Cyclonette (Germany) 63
CZ (Czechoslovakia) 66
Danglard, 76
Davidson, Arthur 19
Davidson, Walter 19

Dayton (Dayton, Ohio U.S.A.) 27
De-Dion Bouton (France) 42, 55, 166
De-Dion, Comte Albert 55
DeRosier, Jake 104
Diey, Yves 235
DKW (Germany) 56, 87
Douglas (England) 53, 93, 102, 145, 156
Dvrandal (France) 99
Easter Holiday 117, 119, 120,1 21, 122, 123, 124, 125, 126, 127, 128
Eclipse Machine Co. 103, 104, 105
Emblem (Angola, New York U.S.A.) 30,82
Enfield Mfg. Co. 140
Excelsior (Chicago, Illinois, U.S.A. 24, 25, 26, 27, 28, 29, 94, 155
Eysink (The Netherlands) 52, 86
Flanders 4, (Detroit, Michigan U.S.A.) 24
Fialiakowski, W, 170, 171
Fleming, Jessie 12
Fleming, Clark 12
Flying Merkel (WI, PA & OH U.S.A.) 39
FN (Belgium) 44, 52, 59, 65, 143, 147
Fongers (The Netherlands) 105
Fossier, Auguste 77
Fossier, Honore' 74
Franklin, Charles 107
Frantisek Janecek 65
Fraser, Alec 99
Garrard, Charles Rilery 78
Gnome & Rhone (France) 60
Goerke, Walter 103
Goldman, Franz 46
Giuppone, 78
Goricke (Germany) 73
Greef, J.W.
Green, G.M. 81
Greyhound (Aurora, Illinois, U.S.A.) 29
Guignard, Paul 74
Harley-Davidson (Milwaukee, Wisconsin, U.S.A.)18, 19, 20, 21, 22, 23, 24, 43, 84, 85, 92, 148, 151, 152, 154, 156, 159, 160, 245
Harley, William 19

INDEX:

Hedstrom, Oscar 15
Hendee, George 15
Henderson (Detroit, Michigan U.S.A.) 28
Henley, Harry 38
Hoffman, Gertrude 21
Husqvarna (Sweden) 67
Hutchinson 81
Huy (Germany) 102
Indian (Springfield, Mass. U.S.A.) 10, 11, 12, 13, 14, 15, 20, 31, 40, 84, 93, 94, 98, 107, 150, 153, 154, 156
Ingram, W. 82
James (Birmingham, England) 48, 164
James, Harold 48
JAP (England) 56, 63, 89
Jawa (Czechoslovakia) 65
Jefferson (Wisconsin, U.S.A.) 29
Komet (Germany) 42, 91
Krampus 133, 134
Kruger, Werner 73
La Francaise-Diamant (France) 99
Lanfranchi, 75
Leon-Bollee (France) 47, 167
LeRoy, Alfred 22
Levis (England) 50
Lincoln-Elk (England) 47
Lipscombe, Guy 99
Luna Park 79
M&M (Massachussetts, U.S.A.) 30, 101, 102. 103
Mars (Germany) 90
Marsh, William 101
Marsh-Metz (MA, U.S.A.) 96
Martin, Franz 72
Merkel, Joseph 39
Metz, Charles 96, 101
Michaelson (Minneapolis, MN U.S.A) 37
Minerva (Belgium) 61, 66
Minneapolis (Minnesota, U.S.A.) 27
Moore, Richard 49
Motobecane (France) 45

Motocomfort (France) 45
Moto Guzzi (Italy) 164
Motorcycle Equipment Co. 100
N.S.U. (Germany) 46, 54, 61
N.U.T. (England) 147
New Hudson (England) 89, 108, 158
New, Richard E. 23
New Year holiday 110, 111, 112, 113, 114, 201
Norton (England) 55
Norton, James Lansdowne 78
Oberewegner, A.R. 82
OEC Temple-JAP (England) 80
Oldfield, Barney 22
Orionette (Germany) 44
P&M (England) 49, 153, 157
Panther (England) 49
Peguy, Charles 73
Pentecost holiday 116
Pernette, 76, 77
Peugeot (France) 76
Phelon, Johah 49
Pierce (Buffalo, New York, U.S.A.) 38
Pope (CT and MA U.S.A.) 32
Pope, Albert Agustus 32
Porteous Butler (France) 43
Premier (England) 53, 55, 56
Prestwich, John Alfred 66
Puch (Austria) 143
Q.
Raleigh (England) 49, 63
Reading Standard (Reading, Pennsylvania U.S.A. 37
Rene-Gillet (France) 88, 141
Rener Repair Co. 10,
Rex (England) 45, 64
Rex Acme Co. 64
Rice, A.C. 104
Risqué, 228, 229
Rodriquez, Gottfried 103
Rosenlocher, Curt 73, 74
Rover (England) 62, 68, 69

INDEX:

Royal Enfield (England, India) 140
Rozos, Carlos 64
Rudge (England) 60, 99
Rudge, Dan 60
Rudge-Whitworth (England) 60, 98
Sagir, Xavier 215
Sarolea (Belgium) 70
Schwinn, Arnold & Co. 26
Schwinn, Ignaz 28
Sears (Chicago, Illinois, U.S.A.) 78
Sebastian, John A 23
Seymour, Raymond 105
Simplex (The Netherlands) 157
Smith Motor Wheel (Milwaukee, Wisconsin U.S.A.) 30
Sokolov, Gligor Ivanov 80
Spencer, J.J. 34
Spencer, Mary Ceoline 34
Spencer, Nellie Elizabeth 34
Spring (Belgium) 67
Starley, James 62
Steib 88, 142
Stevens, A.J. & Co. 69
Styria (Austria) 98
Sulkowsky, Z 95
Sunbeam (England) 53
Tainey, C.B. 37
Taylor, L.S. 78
Terrot, 141 (France)
Thiem (ST. Paul, MN U.S.A.) 28
Thor (Aurora, IL U.S.A.) 33, 34, 40, 78
Triumph (England, Germany) 49, 51, 58, 62, 91, 140, 142
U
Valentines Day 114, 115
Vallee-Picand, W.
Velocette (England) 60
Viratelle (France) 100
Vulcain? (France) 100
Wagner (St. Paul, MN U.S.A.) 35
Wagner, Clara 105
Walker, Ben 84

Wall of Death 81
Walters, Easter 21
Wanderer (Germany) 44, 143
Werner, Michel 75
Werner, Eugene 75
Westfal (Germany) 74
Whittles, Ed 76
Woodman, Miss "Cy" 24
Wright, Curtis 26
Wright, J.S. 80
X
Yale (Toledo Ohio, U.S.A.) 31, 36, 37, 82, 106
Zenith Gradua (England) 50
Zundapp (Germany) 67, 86, 142, 143

POST CARD

Dear Friends,

I hope that you have enjoyed my collection of motorcycle images. These pictures depict scenes from the earliest days of two and three wheel transportation. They have been collected over many years and from many countries. Thanks for enjoying Them with me.

Best Wishes, Jerry

To:
Lovers of vintage motorcycles and postcard images.

FRONT: Jerry Hooker with 1972 R75/5 BMW and Bender Florin sidecar.